THE
POET'S
GUIDE TO
LIFE

THE
POET'S
GUIDE TO
LIFE

The Wisdom of Rilke

Edited and Translated by Ulrich Baer

THE MODERN LIBRARY

NEW YORK

2005 Modern Library Edition

Published in the United States by Modern Library, an imprint of
The Random House Publishing Group, a division of Random House, Inc., New York.

MODERN LIBRARY and the TORCHBEARER Design are registered trademarks of
Random House, Inc.

LIBRARY OF CONGRESS CATALOGING-IN-PUBLICATION DATA
Rilke, Rainer Maria
[Correspondence. English. Selections]
The poet's guide to life: the wisdom of Rilke / Rainer Maria Rilke;
translated, edited, and with an introduction by Ulrich Baer.
p.   cm.
Excerpts in English translation from approximately 7,000
of Rilke's German and French letters.
Includes bibliographical references.
ISBN 0-679-64292-7
1. Rilke, Rainer Maria, 1875–1926—Correspondence.   2. Rilke, Rainer Maria—
Translations into English.   3. Authors, German—20th century—
Correspondence.   I. Baer, Ulrich.   II. Title.
PT2635.I65Z48 2005
831'.912—dc22   2004055990

Modern Library website address: www.modernlibrary.com

Printed in the United States of America on acid-free paper

2 4 6 8 9 7 5 3 1

CONTENTS

INTRODUCTION *by Ulrich Baer*   vii

ON LIFE AND LIVING: *You Have to Live Life to the Limit*   5

ON BEING WITH OTHERS:
To Be a Part, That Is Fulfillment for Us   29

ON WORK: *Get Up Cheerfully on Days You Have to Work*   43

ON DIFFICULTY AND ADVERSITY:
The Measure by Which We May Know Our Strength   55

ON CHILDHOOD AND EDUCATION: *This Joy in Daily Discovery*   65

ON NATURE: *It Knows Nothing of Us*   75

ON SOLITUDE: *The Loneliest People Above All Contribute
Most to Commonality*   81

ON ILLNESS AND RECOVERY: *Pain Tolerates No Interpretation*   93

ON LOSS, DYING, AND DEATH: *Even Time Does Not "Console" . . .
It Puts Things in Their Place and Creates Order*   105

ON LANGUAGE: *That Vast, Humming, and Swinging Syntax*   125

ON ART: *Art Presents Itself as a Way of Life*   133

ON FAITH: *A Direction of the Heart*   161

ON GOODNESS AND MORALITY: *Nothing Good, Once It Has Come into
Existence, May Be Suppressed*   177

ON LOVE: *There Is No Force in the World but Love*   185

SOURCES   203

Ulrich Baer

> But to have been
> *once,* even though only *once:*
> this having been *earthly* seems lasting, beyond repeal.
>
> All that we
> can achieve here, is to recognize ourselves completely
> in what can be seen on earth.
>
> DUINO ELEGIES (NR 9)

E very morning the poet sat down at his desk to work. Every-
thing had been carefully prepared: he had dressed in shirt, tie,
and a dark tailored suit; eaten breakfast at the table (whenever pos-
sible, there was real silver and heavy linen); sipped his good coffee;
and kept most of his language to himself, expending it only to ad-
dress his discreet housekeeper with a brief comment about the
weather or how the cut flowers were nicely holding up. Now he
faced the two pens before him. One pen was reserved for work—
the few volumes of poems that he had published and the single
novel that had won him some acclaim—while the other was the
pen for dispensing with bills, requests, and letters, the sort of things
that required words and language but did not qualify, as far as the

reading public or his own exacting self were concerned, as poetic "work." He had adopted a maxim early in life, during one of his apprenticeships with an older artist whose exemplary focus had been an inspiration: "One must work, nothing but work, and one must have patience." On several occasions, he had cited this maxim in print and had even authored a short book on the artist's work and life. But, in truth, it had not been easy for him to understand how a person could so uncompromisingly privilege work above all else. Alas, how *to live* according to this mantra, which extolled the sanctification of work, proved even harder. Nothing but work. Every morning, face nothing but yourself, be truly alone, and choose between the two pens that could channel the production of the day. There was the desk, carefully placed in the center of the room and lovingly covered with a silk scarf lent by a wealthy friend; there were the flowers sent by the same friend and arranged in a round white vase; there was one stack of expensive "work" paper and another one of equally expensive (really quite indulgent) stationery. Everything was set, he was dressed the part, and now it was only a matter of setting pen to paper and then "nothing but work." But Rilke knew that his maxim was starting to sound as hollow as most daily prayers, and he knew even more acutely that all his trappings were nothing but a disguise, a masquerade to cover up the self-indulgent urge to get up and walk somewhere, go back to bed, to check on the mail or on the roses, to give in to temptation and take a walk, take a call, take a break. Just as he was about to rise from his chair, ready to lose this morning's battle that lasted but seconds and yet tore at his soul, his eyes fell on the small book listing his correspondence. Every letter he received was entered there with name and date, and those to whom he had responded were crossed off.

He would write letter after letter, several of them running up to eight pages in length. The next thing that happened was the housekeeper's gentle tapping on the door. It was lunchtime. A stack of neatly addressed envelopes had risen on the table, and more than two dozen names had been crossed off "the certain little list" in the small book. Had he worked? Which pen had been picked up? For several hours, language had coursed through him as if it were oil or wax that becomes more pliant when subjected to movement and heat. His pen had yielded what he called "the juice": a few of the letters were personal, playful, brimming with witty images, self-mocking asides and details of his everyday life; others barely contained a proper greeting before unfolding an extended and precise reflection on a particular question or problem. Throughout the morning, Rilke had conversed intimately with a series of individuals, ever so slightly inflecting his voice for each of them. In the process of writing his letters, he had advanced not only his thinking but also his language. Since these were letters destined to leave him within hours, however, they served a different function from the journal, diary, and notebooks he kept to jot down drafts and ideas as potential seeds for longer poems. The letters became the rehearsal space of which Rilke lifted the curtain on his creative process just enough to fend off the sense of isolation that threatened to undermine his hard-won and cherished solitude. "In addition to my voice which points beyond me," he writes in a letter of January 24, 1920, "there is still the sound of that small longing which originates in my solitude and which I have not entirely mastered, a whistling-woeful tone that blows through a crack in this leaky solitude—, it *calls out,* alas, and summons others to me!" The work pen had not been touched, no poem had been born, and a few of the sheets reserved only for verse had even been conscripted when the stationery had run out. Pages and pages had been filled. And although Rilke sent these letters out, he had amassed and saved for others the wealth of expressed ideas, striking images, and verbalized thoughts that he would later distill into the denser shapes of his poetic work.

Rainer Maria Rilke's work has captured the imagination of musicians, philosophers, artists, writers, and poetry lovers, and it has extended the reach of poetry to people rarely concerned with human utterances cast in verse. Marlene Dietrich, Martin Heidegger, and Warren Zevon all recited Rilke poems by heart. This capacity of Rilke's words to touch such different people as if each word had been written just for them, aside from his esteem among fellow poets and academics, lends his poetry its force and has saved his work from becoming simply an artifact of the civilization that Hegel first called Old Europe. The power of Rilke's writings results from his capacity to interlock the description of everyday objects, minute feelings, small gestures, and overlooked things— that which makes up the world for each of us—with transcendent themes. By interlocking the everyday and the transcendent, Rilke suggests in his poetry, and minutely explains in his letters, that the key to the secrets of our existence might be found right in front of our eyes. This suggestion is not solely the province of Rilke's poetry, which amounts to eleven collections published before his death in 1926 and a large number of posthumously published poems. He was a prodigious letter writer, and in his astoundingly vast correspondence Rilke let go of the constraints of German verse to produce powerful and accessible reflections on a vast range of topics.

Treat this book like a user's manual for life: open it anywhere, if what you need right now is the grounding for your experience that seems lacking during especially trying or exhilarating periods of our lives. Or use *The Poet's Guide to Life* as an adaptable resource for the moments in life when something meaningful deserves to be said. For good reason, the relatively scant number of Rilke's words so far available in English have already become perennial favorites at weddings and graduation ceremonies, and they are placed on the walls of hospitals and nursery schools. Rilke possessed the uncanny ability to phrase the most profound experiences and emotions with great precision and without detaching them from the lived reality in which they arise or to which they respond. This book contains these words, which Rilke intended to be *used in and for life*. He did not want his writing to be put under glass like orchids made of silk but instead hoped it would be read irreverently, spoken not only by professional custodians of high culture, but breathed deeply into the messiness of life that no one can avoid.

Rilke points out that we can be shaken by losses and by gains, that we may be unsettled as much by negative encounters, adversity, difficulty, illness, loss, and death as by the peculiar intensification of our being in the experience of joy, friendship, creation, and, especially, love. He also stresses that during those experiences, even when they bring us closer to others, we are fundamentally alone. During such moments, when our life is suddenly open to questioning, we are cast back on ourselves without support from any outside agency. Every rite of passage—birth, adolescence, love, commitment, illness, loss, death—marks such an experience where we are faced with our solitude. But this is not a melancholic thought for Rilke. He revalorizes solitude as the occasion to reconsider our decisions and experiences, and to understand ourselves more accurately—and his words can serve as uncannily apt guides for such reflection.

If you are looking for specific guidance when your life confronts or rewards you with a particular challenge or opportunity, then go to a specific section. This book is organized in sections that match the overarching themes I found in the roughly seven thousand letters by Rilke I have read. The sequence of chapters and the excerpts within each chapter is not chronological but based on my experience of reading Rilke's work. It maps life on a trajectory that leads from a consideration of being with others, work, adversity, education, nature, and solitude through illness, loss, and death to the emergence of ourselves into language, art, creation, and, finally, the culmination of ourselves in the experience of love. Oh, yes, Rilke is the great poet of love. He was not born that way, but his own experiences left him with no choice but to believe without surrender in that great, excessive possibility of loving another human being, which might befall any one of us at any moment. But, no, he is not sentimental. Love is placed at the end of this book because for Rilke love is work and, ultimately, a difficult achievement of the soul. In our age that is so hungry for spiritual sustenance and so easily seduced by the promise of salvation, Rilke proves relevant by defining love as modern man's equivalent of the prayer to our vanished gods. It is the great gift that the otherwise radically indifferent if not inhospitable world can bestow on us— in the form of the encounter with another person. This is not an easy thing to phrase correctly. And there are countless other instances of small or vast internal shifts, which sometimes, but not always, coincide with socially marked and widely celebrated life events, that can benefit from the lucidity of Rilke's prose. *The Poet's Guide to Life* is meant to offer words that can capture the significance, the depth, the import of such occasions.

Rilke's *Letters to a Young Poet* (a series of ten letters written between 1903 and 1908 and first published in 1929) have initiated scores of readers into a serious engagement with Rilke, while the famous opening of the *Duino Elegies*—"Who, if I cried out, would hear me scream among the angels' orders?"—undoubtedly ranks among the most poignant expressions of man's thirst for meaning in an age bereft of transcendental assurances. To the same degree that Rilke has compelled readers outside of the academy, literary critics produce lengthy analyses of Rilke's promise of redemption suspended over the abyss of nothingness which haunts all of modern literature. This promise of existential salvation in Rilke's work is considered the extreme possibility of modern, that is, secular, literature.

And yet, while there has been remarkably sustained interest in and productive critical engagement with his work, the Rilke of everyday life is waiting to be discovered. The famous *Letters to a Young Poet* constitutes nothing but a small fragment of Rilke's true output as a letter writer. That slim book was written during a period when Rilke was still searching for his way as a poet and had barely begun to live the life that would lend his correspondence its poignancy, intensity, and weight. In those ten early letters, Rilke elaborately advises a younger poet to wait patiently for his proper calling but does not offer a nuanced view of what such a life would actually *feel* like, nor how we may deal with those parts of life that call us away from our desks and studies and stubbornly, gloriously, painfully distract us from this somewhat idealized, monkish devotion to our task.

This other Rilke, presented here for the first time in English, is an accessible, insightful, and, above all, surprisingly *aware* man who maintained an enormous, indeed staggering, correspondence with a vast array of people including aristocrats and cleaning ladies, shop owners and politicians, his wife, various patrons, editors, friends, lovers, fellow poets and artists, and unknown admirers. He responded invariably to a letter regardless of the sender's station if he felt that the mailing, even from an unknown individual, "spoke to him." In the excerpts selected for this book, Rilke reveals his thoughts about political revolutions, the role of god for modern man, the Catholic Church, Islam and religion in general, and the medical profession. He expounds on love and life; on sickness, death, and loss; on childhood, difficulties, adversity, joys, and work; on belief and art and language; and on friendship, marriage, and simply being with others.

There is something exhilarating about reading Rilke's letters and witnessing Rilke's mind simultaneously at ease and at work. We discover an unknown side of Rilke through his letters. Although he was an innovator and iconoclast in verse, Rilke's letters are ultimately more urgent performances because they were not intended to reach the educated, poetry-reading public as a new set of self-consciously modernist, sublimely sculpted artworks. In the letters, Rilke searches out every angle of that celebrated inner life from which his poetry is born and which presents many readers, when they encounter it in Rilke's precise yet accessible prose, with the startling insight that they, too, possess more interiority than they had assumed. Only readers who jealously guard Rilke as the domain of poetry experts alone or who are tethered to the porcelain figure of Rilke-the-sage-of-golden-afternoon-wisdom will profess surprise at the real-life applicability—yes, even *usefulness*—of his frequently trenchant observations in the correspondence. For there exists a fundamental continuity between Rilke's exhorting the readers of his poetry to experience life as if each moment were something new and his tough-minded and lucid analysis of the human condition in his letters creating space for this exact appreciation of existence.

The Poet's Guide to Life presents for the first time in English translation excerpts chosen from Rilke's roughly seven thousand German and French letters in print (his total correspondence, still waiting for publication and, in some cases, the expiration of copyrights held by addressees, is estimated to encompass about eleven thousand letters). In his last will, Rilke declared every single one of his letters to be as much a part of his work as each of his many poems, and he authorized publication of the entire correspondence. But before this official legitimation of his daily writing as part of the oeuvre, his letters' recipients had long grasped that they held in their hands another Rilke whose voice rivaled in significance that heard in the poetry. Already at the age of seventeen, Rilke had professed a preference for writing letters over verse to reach his addressee in ways not secured by poetry: "I could tell you all of this in verse—and although verses have become second nature to me, the artless, simple—but richly expressive word [of a letter] issues more easily from my heart—to reach your heart," he writes on May 2, 1893, to his first love Valery von David-Rhonfeld. In this poignant distinction between letters and verse, Rilke coyly suggests that his beloved recipient calls forth his turn to prose. The irony, of course, is that if poetry had become Rilke's "second nature," the letters were now more valued according to Rilke himself because they occasioned new and unexpected expressions. More significantly, Rilke's desire to reach his addressee without artifice or rhetoric emerges here: when Rilke has something urgent and intimate to impart, he takes recourse to the "artless, simple" letter rather than verse. Indeed all of Rilke's letters, and not only this early instance, originate in the desire to address the other directly as "you." Whereas his poetry reaches far beyond any calculable recipient, his letters invite and locate the other within what Rilke calls the "ever-widening circles" of his existence. By attributing to his letters a different capacity for reaching the other, Rilke reveals to his recipients, with as much force as his poetry but less burdened by the formal conventions of the lyric, what could be meant by a *guide to life.*

Rilke's Life: 1875–1926

A guide to life: what could this mean? And what could it mean to be guided by someone whose biography, which has become a shimmering myth in itself, does not exactly provide an example to be emulated? Rilke left his wife and child to become a poet and initiated passionate affairs with several women only to end those relationships when he felt the urge to return to his desk. He often overspent on his modest income from publications and lecturing and was forced to plead with and occasionally beg from benefactors and his publisher for advances, grants, cash gifts, and emergency loans. He was extremely sensitive to criticism, and though princesses, politicians, Europe's most famous writers and countless enchanted readers heaped him with praise, one slight from an unknown individual could unsettle him profoundly. He abhorred organized religion and distrusted the medical profession; he died of undiagnosed leukemia in 1926, after suffering unnecessarily because he refused all but the most basic medication. And as much as he cherished solitude and independence, Rilke relied so heavily on the kindness of patrons that some moralizing biographers have scolded him for the distasteful bourgeois craving to belong to upper-crust society into which he had not been born and whose privileges he could not afford.

Rilke was born in 1875 in Prague to socially ambitious middle-class German-speaking parents whose lives never amounted to what they had envisioned for themselves. He was slated for the type of military career that his father abandoned in great frustration after failing to be promoted, but he dropped out of military academy after suffering for several years in the strict environment. He gained his high school diploma by studying with tutors, and by the age of twenty had published two volumes of poetry, edited a small literary journal, and fallen passionately in love with Valery. After a year at the university studying art history, literature, and philosophy, he fled the narrowness of Prague (also home to Franz Kafka and Franz Werfel, both of whom Rilke greatly admired) for Munich, where he continued his studies for another year. He resolved to become a poet and embarked on a period of emotional and artistic apprenticeships in the form of long trips to Italy and Russia with his lover Lou Andreas-Salomé, the older and far more worldly woman to whom Friedrich Wilhelm Nietzsche had once proposed marriage and who would be among the first female psychoanalysts trained by Sigmund Freud. Andreas-Salomé mentored and mothered Rilke and encouraged him to change his name René to the more masculine Rainer, and to practice a signature and penmanship with the verve and flourish befitting a poet. Lou proved a good teacher: already during his lifetime many of Rilke's elegantly printed books bore no title but only an embossed facsimile of his carefully designed, seamless, flowing *Rainer Maria Rilke* . Rilke traveled widely, met and fell in love with a young German sculptor, Clara Westhoff, and married her in April 1901 after she had become pregnant with their only daughter, Ruth, who would be born in December of the same year. After a year of living on very little money in a rustic farm house in northern Germany with Clara and their daughter,

Rilke left his young family for the bright lights of Paris where he finagled a position as office assistant for the sculptor Auguste Rodin. Clara joined him in Paris for a while after leaving their daughter to be raised by her parents, but Rilke never returned to live with his family. While Clara remained a friend and Rilke conscientiously paid the living expenses of his wife and daughter throughout his life, he knew full well that he had been neither a good husband nor was ever a good father.

The years in Paris proved formative. Rilke became a well-known poet in German-speaking countries after publishing several volumes of verse, including *The Book of Hours* in 1905 (a series of immensely vivid prayers to god written with the fervor and swagger of an adolescent boy burning up with unconsummated, pent-up longing for real love) and the decisively modernist *New Poems* in 1909. In the latter collection, Rilke perfected his genre of linguistic still lifes, *Dinggedichte,* or "thing-poems," which present a series of objects' effects on the poet's consciousness (rather than chronicling the poet's emotional or cognitive responses to them). Extensive travels took him to Russia; various parts of Europe, including Italy, Spain, and parts of Scandinavia; and northern Africa, including Morocco and Egypt. With the outbreak of World War I, Rilke was drafted into the Austro-Hungarian army. After an initial burst of enthusiasm for the war (Rilke was no pacifist but believed in the occasional necessity of military intervention to secure peace), he sought help from well-placed friends who eventually secured a writing assignment for him at a safe remove from the front. During this period, his poetic writing all but ceased. Rilke had been forced to leave Paris as an enemy-citizen with no time to plan and no certainty of a return date; he lost all of his belongings with the exception of two trunks filled with papers that André Gide tracked down and secured for him until after the war. He shuttled between Munich and Vienna waiting for his draft notification and then, after his service, for his army release. A photograph from this time shows the poet's large head as a gaunt, frozen mask with a look of resignation as if there were nothing left in the world that could elicit a response from him. For Rilke, this state of emotional numbness was the worst possible fate; his true compassion (and self-pity) always extended to those for whom the world had ceased to provide a new experience.

Rilke left Germany in 1919 and never again set foot in the country where he enjoyed the greatest reputation. His books were published there, but he felt deep ambivalence toward Germany and held it responsible for the devastating war and its aftermath. "How *very much* I hate this people [the Germans] . . . Nobody will ever be able to claim that I write in *their* language!" Rilke writes, in German, on January 1, 1923. Aside from translations during the war years, Rilke largely stopped writing poetry until 1922, when wealthy patrons bought and modestly restored a somewhat dilapidated, small stone cottage (though bearing the title "château") in Switzerland where he could recover from the war years' psychic wounds. He also fell in love again, and again, and then another time—for many women, Rilke proved utterly irresistible, and often he chose not to put up any defenses. In 1912—a decade earlier—Rilke had begun writing his *Duino Elegies* in the old castle of Duino, near Trieste, on the rugged northern Italian coast owned by his close friends, the prince and princess of Thurn and Taxis. In 1923, Rilke finished the *Elegies* and wrote his *Sonnets to Orpheus* in a burst of exceptional creativity over a two-week period in February in the tower of Muzot. Muzot had become more than a safe haven: it was now the temple where his greatest poetic creation was conceived, and Switzerland would be the place of refuge from which he would never again leave. Rilke completed the ten long *Elegies* (an additional eleventh elegy was ultimately excluded) in eight days and wrote the first twenty-five poems in *Sonnets to Orpheus* between February 2 and February 5, 1923, and then completed the fifty-five-poem cycle, in addition to a series of uncollected poems, in another ten days one week later. Even some of Rilke's detractors grudgingly conceded that in the case of Rilke's self-described "hurricane of most intense abilities," during which the *Elegies* and *Sonnets* had been written, the "bourgeois myth" of the inspired genius for once held true.

Biographers have seized on the absence of publications during the war years, until the completion of the *Elegies,* to portray Rilke as a sickly, suffering figure too fragile and too pure for this world. But Rilke was not silent by any means between 1914 and 1922. For nearly a decade, he had refined his language and his thinking by writing countless—probably over a thousand—letters that opened up the space where the poems could gestate. Much more than mere notes to his poems, Rilke's letters reveal the movement of his thought before it is condensed and compacted into metaphor and verse. When Rilke looked back at the war years in 1925, he reflected on the "grace" of having preserved his own ability to write poetry as a sign of *everyone's* capacity to be rescued from the blows dealt by fate: this grace is "more than only a private experience because it constitutes a measure for the inexhaustible layering of our nature that, by proving that it may be possible to continue, could peculiarly console many who had considered themselves internally devastated for different reasons." This sense of having overcome great adversity informs all of his letters. They offer eloquent proof that his wartime silence was only partial and constitute a significant and substantive "layer" of Rilke's nature.

From 1922 until his death from leukemia in 1926, Rilke lived in relative seclusion in Switzerland for long periods between friends' visits, short trips, and spells of illness. When Paul Valéry, whom Rilke revered and whose style he emulated in a late collection of poems written in French, visited Rilke's tower he was bewildered how anyone could choose to live in such isolation. Rilke maintained his frequent correspondence with literally hundreds of people while in Switzerland and kept on writing even through the increasingly severe pain of his undiagnosed cancer. His patrons and supporters, ranging from Europe's aristocrats to industrialists, businessmen, and heirs of trading fortunes, professed a seemingly unshakable faith in his capacity to produce; their occasional worries about lavishing money on a poet who failed to publish a book for over a decade and who had a habit of staying for extended periods in hotels he could not at all afford, are directly addressed and alleviated in Rilke's letters. Most of these letters are so personal and lucid that one imagines the mere arrival of such well-put wisdom to be sufficient recompense for the money Rilke received. Indeed, all of his correspondents realized that with each letter they were given something that would far outlast anything bought with their money (which did not keep some of them from putting these letters on the auction block before Rilke was dead). In other letters, Rilke painstakingly explains—and thus also reassures himself—that the creative process needs peace and time unencumbered by guilt and pressure to produce and that even during periods of stagnation and apparent indolence an artist might be preparing internally what will emerge only later as his "work." Early in his life Rilke was blessed to find a shrewd and endlessly supportive editor and publisher, Anton Kippenberg, the founder of Germany's Insel Verlag, where Rilke is still published today. He made some of Rilke's short prose available in inexpensive and quickly best-selling small books, returned all of his poetry to print during his lifetime, and wisely managed both Rilke's money and his increasingly influential and consequently sought-after name by limiting permissions for anthologies and prepublication in journals. In his lifetime, Rilke enjoyed the passionate interest of numerous readers and critics. Only briefly in the early 1920s did his star threaten to dim slightly when his style of emotionally intense and dignified poetry had to compete with the shock effects of expressionism, surrealism, and Dadaism. (A similar brief decline in Rilke's popularity occurred in Germany for a few years after 1968, when more overtly political poetry was en vogue and Rilke was branded a gilded icon of the bourgeoisie.)

Rilke's life seems to have followed a rhythm whose beats are somewhat more widely spaced than the empirical events listed by biographers: publications, grants, reviews, and accolades; friendships, loves, and losses; trips, moves, and encounters with notables of his day. The details of his biography—his series of lovers, his military service, his travels, his complex relationships with donors, his engagement with the artists of his time—though fascinating individually, are ultimately subsumed into a greater cadence, a more expansive beat that often gets obscured by the details of most existing biographies. This greater cadence steadily pervades Rilke's lines in both poetry and prose like the focused, silent breathing of a great yogi. In his poetry and prose, Rilke links through various images the affairs of human life to the movements of the cosmos itself. If this conceit seems hyperbolic, it is for Rilke rooted very deeply in his experiences of the world. The result is not esoteric, nor does it relativize and thus implicitly belittle human activity by placing it within a greater, superior—not divine—order. By seeing things rather within a larger, natural (rather than ideological or re-

ligious) pattern, Rilke achieves a fundamentally modern secu-
lar perspective but does not give up on the possibility that there
might be something greater in our lives. Interestingly, Rilke finds
evidence of a connectedness to larger, cosmic patterns within our
physical, bodily existence. How we breathe, eat, sleep, digest, and
love; how we suffer physically or experience pleasure: we are sub-
ject to rhythms we cannot totally control. Rilke relies on no idea-
tional frame but understands our existence as that of decidedly
earthly, embodied mortals or, in the language of the philosophers
whose work he so significantly shaped and inspired, as beings in
time.

Rilke can sound like a visionary when he writes on love. This
is well known. When he explains how one might act during or
after a serious disagreement in a marriage, or how a person may act
on his or her attraction to someone of the same sex, however, he is
rewardingly pragmatic, applicable, and decisively progressive. This
is something nearly unknown to most of his readers: in his outlook
on society and politics as evidenced by the letters, Rilke was a so-
cial progressive; some may consider him a radical. His views on art
are no less advanced. They constitute an important counterpoint to
both the romantic image of the poet as the "Santa Claus of loneli-
ness" (W. H. Auden's description of Rilke) and to an increasingly
pervasive understanding of art during his lifetime in the terms dic-
tated by the entertainment industries, the publishing business, and
the art market. And when he explains the process of creation, per-
haps slightly overstating his admiration for a patron's success in
commerce, he explains why he considers even the art of the deal to
be an important and worthwhile pursuit in human terms. When
he addresses such prosaic topics, he is persuasive precisely because
he was not immune to, and consequently had true insight into,

how life is lived today, which includes a keen, painfully achieved understanding of the business world and the rewards and pitfalls of public recognition.

Rilke's Worldview in His Letters

In his poetry, Rilke's deft intermingling of narrowly focused and expansive perspectives may take the form of the governing metaphor of "falling," which allows him to present as a continuous movement the falling of the autumn's leaves, our own inevitable falling and demise, and the great and directionless falling of our planet through the vastness of space. In the letters, Rilke accounts for this expansive, space-creating rhythm in which he sought to place our understanding of life by addressing all the things that could not be properly assimilated at the time of their occurrence. To view things as part of an expanded perspective meant for him to acknowledge and live through the depth of their difficulty rather than try to eradicate them or spew them out on a psychoanalyst's couch "in chunks of the unusable or misunderstood remnants of childhood." For someone like him committed to living the examined life, the only way to conduct this inspection was to write about it. "Time," he writes in another letter, "even time itself does not 'console,' as people say superficially; at best it puts things in their place and creates order." The guidance offered by Rilke, then, is not a quick fix but an adjustment that requires work, participation, mindfulness, and patience.

Rilke was not just serious but often ruthless about carving space for writing out of the marble of the day. "I know that I cannot cut my life out of the fates with which it has grown intertwined," Rilke writes in a 1903 letter to Andreas-Salomé about his decision to leave his wife and young child, "but I have to find the strength to lift life in its entirety and including everything into calmness, into solitude, into the quiet of profound days of labor." Rilke was too preoccupied with his work to make a good father or husband. A "guide to life" does not have to be established by example. Rilke himself preempted his critics' tendency to focus on his biography and pass judgment on his life, with its damning decisions, difficulties, and sublime achievements, by deferring every question about it to his art. In anticipation of the judgment of later critics and biographers about the choices in his life, Rilke referred everyone close to him "to those regions where he had cast all of his talents": his art. Yes, Rilke occasionally invoked his "calling to art" as an excuse for his failures. Yet he wanted to make absolutely sure that the way he lived was only to be determined by him. It is precisely this realization that lends his words their strength:

> Do not believe that the person who is trying to offer you solace lives his life effortlessly among the simple and quiet words that might occasionally comfort you. His life is filled with much hardship and sadness, and it remains far behind yours. But if it were otherwise, he could never have found these words.

The force of Rilke's counsel results from his determination to find the most precise words for what weighs on him and, as he puts it elsewhere, what twists and "deforms" him. His letters capture these dents and impressions left by the torque of life, and because of Rilke's exceptionally fine-tuned ear and unusual willingness to explore his failings they attain great acuity.

The words in Rilke's letters are *lived words,* in the sense in which we sometimes speak of *lived experience:* each word is something that Rilke considered having undergone and, indeed, suffered through. But every word in the letters leads straight back into life, placing the writer and his recipients inside ever-widening circles that know of no outside, beyond, or transcendent greater whole.

Rilke's commitment not to avoid but to become cognizant of the contours of our difficulty finds its parallel in his views on art. His work does not constitute an aesthetic education where the appreciation of beauty leads one to recognize the truth. In the following excerpt from a letter, Rilke parts ways with the Romantic tradition defined by Friedrich Schiller and John Keats:

> You know that what appears inexorable must be present [in poetry] for the sake of our greatest desires. Beauty will become paltry and insignificant when one looks for it only in what is pleasing; there it might be found occasionally but it resides and lies awake in each thing where it encloses itself, and it emerges only for the individual who believes that it is present everywhere and who will not move on until he has stubbornly coaxed it forth.

Beauty "dwells and is awake in each thing": For Rilke, the search for beauty blocks our path to the true purpose of art, which is truth, or integrity and honesty, as he prefers to say. We must look *everywhere,* including in sites that strike us as unpleasant; in his life, similarly, he could not pretend to ignore the parts that did not make sense, hurt him or others badly, or that he would rather have denied, repressed, and forgotten—hence the large number of letters written to his wife, and his effort to understand himself as both an artist and a father. Rilke also ended the Romantic myth that the

body must be given up in a feverish and ecstatic surrender as a sac-
rifice to art. Yes, Rilke had a body (he was of slight build, medium
height, and considered himself homely), and he did not forget its
needs when he was living the life of the mind: "You know that I
am not one of those individuals who neglect their body in order to
turn it into an offering for their soul; my soul would not at all have
appreciated such a sacrifice." He tried to listen to his body and
translate its idiom into intelligible words. And he eschewed the se-
ductions of ironic detachment and self-declared irrelevance in-
dulged in by the modern masters. Without writing, Rilke's letters
suggest, we might fail to grasp what exactly happens and become
numb to reality itself; we might accept the obvious and latent hier-
archies around us and unwittingly acquiesce to unjust conditions,
owing not to cowardice but to our failure to find meaningful ex-
pressions for them, and thus make them apparent to us. His search
for the "simple and quiet words," then, does not amount to qui-
etism. "This having been *earthly* seems lasting, beyond repeal," we
find in the *Elegies.* There is nothing resigned about this statement.
Rather, Rilke's sense that one's mere presence on this planet de-
serves affirmation fueled his commitment to search his experiences
for a guide to life.

For this reason, Rilke attempted to cast himself in words: he had
an urgent need to testify to his life in this world. "How is it possible
to live since the elements of this life remain completely ungraspable
for us?" Rilke asks in another letter. To the daunting nature of life
and its difficulties, Rilke's correspondence is itself an answer.

> The longer I live, the more urgent it seems to me to endure and
> transcribe the whole dictation of existence up to its end, for it
> might just be the case that only the very last sentence contains

that small and possibly inconspicuous word through which every-
thing we had struggled to learn and everything we had failed to
understand will be transformed into magnificent sense.

To transcribe "the whole dictation of existence," Rilke renders in-
telligible to himself what seemed incomprehensible, enigmatic,
unassimilable. He makes a dogged effort to capture every last little
thing without deciding in advance its ultimate significance, be-
tween what may matter and what might leave but a smudge on the
great scroll of being. The will "to endure" also means putting his
preferences and needs aside, capturing his experience in words that
will resonate increasingly as distractions fall away.

So far, and especially for English-speaking readers, this testi-
mony has been limited to Rilke's poetry; his single novel, *The
Notebooks of Malte Laurids Brigge;* and a published fraction of his
correspondence. Some of the poetry has earned Rilke the reputa-
tion as a difficult poet of transcendence. But already in the *The
Book of Hours* of 1903, Rilke is an amazingly direct heretic. If a
poem such as "I live my life in widening circles / I circle around
god, the ancient tower" still seems theocentric, the impiety of
Rilke's utterly self-crafted and hard-won belief becomes evident in
these lines from the same collection: "What will you do, god,
when I am dead? / In losing me you lose your meaning." Rilke be-
lieved that we may gain access to something beyond ourselves
within and *through* ourselves rather than by reaching a higher power
that supersedes and thus ultimately minimizes our own potential—
the way an arrow on a taut bowstring is "*more* / than itself at the
moment just before release," or how "love is nothing but the urgent
and blessed appeal for another person to be beautiful, abundant,
great, intense, unforgettable; nothing but the surging commitment
for him to amount to something."

The image of Rilke as a poet of transcendence is as much a misunderstanding as the clichés of Rilke the healer; the self-indulgent scribe of solitude; the patron saint of adolescent angst; the seraphic, infirm poet crushed by the world. The most comprehensive "dictation" of Rilke's existence, where he might discover that "small and inconspicuous" word that will suddenly transform everything into "magnificent sense," as he puts it, occurs in his correspondence. These letters present Rilke's wisdom without the patina of learnedness that has covered his verse over the years or the anecdotes that have encrusted it with biographical tidbits. These letters sparkle with insight and originality, they produce utterly unexpected turns of thought, and they converse with us: they are anything but monumental. Unavailable in English until now, they unsettle the ossified public image of Rilke as a slightly aloof, pseudo-aristocratic author of inspirational verse. And because many of them have become public only very recently and long after their recipients' deaths, they reach us by and large as their actual, first readers.

Rilke often felt that he was held back, like a failing student, in the "pain-classes of life." Although he had dropped out of military academy, Rilke remained a disciplined student even in life, and when threatened with flunking its "pain-classes" he set upon deciphering and studying for the hard lessons again. For this purpose, he wrote out each "assignment" dealt to him by life in order not to miss anything the next time around—hence some of Rilke's notoriously self-pitying complaints, but hence also his tireless energy in returning to particular questions of our existence to find with each new sentence a more precise way of addressing what remains unanswered. Much of Rilke's strength as a letter writer rests with his particular way of fusing metaphysical thoughts with utterly immediate images. It is true that a good number of these startling contractions of the earthly and the transcendental into a single striking image are the result of sudden inspiration. Many of Rilke's greatest poems were conceived on walks and jotted down outside; the eighth and ninth of the *Duino Elegies,* Rilke wrote to a friend, were completed on the way back from the post office where he had just mailed the "victory" telegram announcing completion of the circle's first seven poems. But the moving images that captured his imagination so suddenly had often germinated as a phrase or image in a letter. Through this unending process of rendering intelligible to himself this life with its afflictions and advantages, with selfish decisions and moments of boundless generosity, Rilke begins to explain life to us.

Rilke diligently rewrote whole pages of his letters while at his custom-built high desk if there was so much as a spelling error or a tiny ink spot on a page, and he began anew whenever his train of thought had been interrupted and he was dissatisfied with the result. But this epistolary perfectionism does not get in the way of accessibility or mitigate each letter's apparently effortless beauty. Even when he wrote dozens of letters in a single day, no two descriptions of the same event are quite the same; for each correspondent, Rilke varied his diction to come closer to the honesty, the precision, and the emotional accuracy he valued above all else in his work. A little over a year before his death in a Swiss sanatorium, Rilke stipulated in October 1925 that his letters could be published "because for several years now I have made it my habit to channel occasionally part of the productivity of my nature into letters." In the letters excerpted here, Rilke hones his power of expression and gradually achieves the acuity and economy that characterizes his poetry. Carrying on his startlingly vast correspondence constituted for Rilke "the ascent into a state of conscious reflection" and a "coming to his senses" as a poet. The letters are Rilke's workshop, laboratory, and rehearsal space where he develops his particular gift of using German to express matters of tremendous gravity—the suffering and the joy promised by life—without turning abstract, turgid, or academic.

In many letters, Rilke creates phrases, thoughts, and descriptions that later enter into a poem. The experience of hearing a birdcall with such immediacy that it seemed to resonate *inside* of him one winter night in Capri finds expression in several letters before it enters two later poems and a prose piece in 1913 (and is quoted by Robert Downey Jr. and Marisa Tomei, to good effect, in the romantic film comedy *Only You*). In another letter written on December 15, 1906, Rilke states his ambition to be able to describe a rose and then gently unfurls a yellow rose for two pages, petal by petal, word by word, lid by lid: a prose rendition of Rilke's favorite flower that doubtlessly prepared the soil for several series of poems on roses written between 1915 and 1921 and, finally, for the haunting epitaph written in 1925 for his own gravestone (the last line plays on the German word *Lied,* which can sound like both *song* and *lid;* the word for "pure" [*reiner*] in the first line is a homonym of his name): "Rose, oh pure [*reiner*] contradiction / joy to be nobody's sleep / beneath so many lids [*Liedern*]."

Frequently, however, as if these descriptions had served only to jolt Rilke's imagination, he does not forsake the letter for a poem but advances to the kind of coherent paragraph where a thought attains relevance for readers beyond the letter's addressee. But because these paragraphs originate in Rilke's epistolary dialogues where he talks about his experiences, they remain grounded in everyday life, and Rilke's awareness of the addressee keeps the prose from becoming abstract or overly general, either of which would make it lose its personal urgency. As if unconsciously signaling the greater relevance of such sections, Rilke rarely uses "I" and almost never addresses his recipient directly when he embarks on a more sweeping reflection or seeks to phrase advice more carefully; the tone detaches from the intimacy of a private letter but involves the other in a dialogue that is neither self-consciously artful nor aloof.

In his letters, Rilke achieves what his aesthetic principles also mandate for true art: all things and experiences are allowed to speak to him from their proper place in the world, and not only as they are framed there and made sense of by him. Just as he invests his poetry with the power to intertwine everyday affairs and transcendent ideas, Rilke writes in a letter that the essence of true help, for instance, might consist in a modest piece of string offered at the right moment, when it's truly needed. This little piece of string could be "no less helpful in saving our strength" than the most elaborate, long-term assistance. For Rilke, both his artistic credo and his most fundamental insight into how to live one's life call for a wholly inclusive view of the world.

There courses through Rilke's work the steady commitment to celebrate life in all of its manifestations. This desire is announced already in the title of one of his first books of poetry, *To Celebrate Myself* (1899). It differs fundamentally from the willingness to get to the bottom of life by any means that characterized poets such as Baudelaire, Verlaine, and Rimbaud against whom the young Rilke defined himself. The point became not to observe and comment on life, describing it as if from the outside, or to wrestle it to the ground and overwhelm it with the aid of intoxicants and provocation. Rilke considered the writer's task to consist of joining his voice to the sounds of agony, suffering, ecstasy, and exhilaration and also to the everyday exchanges between individuals, and the interior monologues of all of us.

Rilke's descriptions of sites, people, and objects achieve a simplicity and analytic precision that Rilke found nowhere in the learned European cultures of which he was a part. By honing his receptivity, attentiveness, and mindfulness, he eschews the shortcuts of received opinion. Instead of tethering himself to a rigid work ethic, however, Rilke sought to bring all of his experiences, including unproductive periods of "infertility" and "idleness," into one uninterrupted state of mind. Like all major writers, he creates from an inchoate awareness of the inadequacy of all available explanations of the world but does not allow this frustration to become the focus of his inquiry and thus drown out the world a second time. Nothing that Rilke read made sufficient sense of his life for him. As a consequence, he wrote a guide to life himself.

> So much has been written (both well and poorly) about things that the things themselves no longer hold an opinion but appear only to mark the imaginary point of intersection for certain clever theories. Whoever wants to say anything about them speaks in reality only about the views of his predecessors and lapses into a semipolemical spirit that stands in exact opposition to the naïve productive spirit with which each object wants to be grasped and understood.

In addition to serving as the workshop for his poetry, then, Rilke's letters claim a perspective on the world that breaks with traditions of knowledge handed down to him. Because in his correspondence Rilke hopes to reach individuals of varying perspective and backgrounds, he often invents several ways of expressing similar or even identical thoughts. To be heard by his correspondents, Rilke abandons established ways of saying things and in this process deepens and frequently expands his own insights and his language. Some of the passages in Rilke's letters are so vibrant, creative, and rhetorically animated because there Rilke surprised himself with a discovery that could not have been planned.

> Wherever an individual's philosophy develops into a system, I experience the almost depressing feeling of a limitation, of a deliberate effort. I try to encounter the human each time at *that* point where the wealth of his experiences still realizes itself in many disparate and distinct ways without coherence and without being curtailed by the limitations and concessions that systematic orders ultimately require.

Rilke's willingness to recognize all facets of existence and experience without relying on any metatheoretical framework, as provided by theology or the humanities, results in a double focus. On one level, there is Rilke's unceasing and yet patient quest to determine what allows us to assume that life might have a meaning beyond our mere material existence. And, as a contrapuntal theme, there is his equally diligent dedication to account for the irreducible uniqueness of existence and thus also precisely for the physical and material aspects of our being in the world. Rilke was attuned to two different melodies (a metaphor for poetry of which he was fond): one a cosmic bass line underscoring all creation and the other a melody that consists of the chatter and talk of everyday people in common situations. In his letters, he succeeds in achieving unusual harmonies composed of these two very different lines: he can be talky and transcendent in the same phrase, at once full of deep wisdom and subtle irony in one paragraph.

The center and heart of Rilke's letters are his reflections on love and death (the heart, of course, being one of Rilke's essential metaphors and literal concerns: possibly more than other poets, Rilke felt that rhymed language links us in fundamental ways to the biorhythms of lung and heart). Love and death, of course, are also the great themes of Rilke's poetry. In his novel *The Notebooks of Malte Laurids Brigge,* completed after his first long stay in Paris in 1908 and meant to record the experience of survival in that disorienting, alienating, and yet abundantly alive city, the narrator begins with the startling matter-of-fact observation that "people come here to die." (No less startling for a book of such profound reflections on death and loss of innocence in modernity is the fact that the first entry written in 1907 is marked, in an uncanny coincidence sometimes achieved by literature, "September 11th, Rue Toullier.") The book ends with a retelling of the biblical parable of the prodigal son who spurns conventional love for a kind of infinite striving of the heart that cannot know any aim, object, or end. In Rilke's rendition, the prodigal son's project becomes that of loving without an object—to love for love's sake. To transcend the ego does not mean, for Rilke, to enter into a spiral of radical self-doubt and philosophical skepticism or to open the floodgates of unconscious desire and irrationality. It means to be swept up by the movement of one's heart (or soul, if you like, or serotonin levels) without ever reaching a state where this movement will lose its purpose and desire by being fulfilled. In the *Elegies,* this thought is expressed in a tone that mixes urgency with earthliness.

Sometimes, however, life alone is urgent enough, and we may not need any more intensity. Instead, what many of us want is what Rilke calls, in a letter of February 10, 1922, "space for the spirit to breathe." This is where the letters come in. They express in striking yet accessible images Rilke's conviction that "our heart always exceeds us" (second *Duino Elegy*) and give us precisely that "space for the spirit to breathe" with a patience, mindfulness, and near serenity that befits a conversation between individuals who have trust and hope in each other but are not encumbered by too much intimacy (or baggage, as we may phrase it today).

These letters also introduce us to refreshingly un-Rilkean metaphors. In describing a disappointing return visit to his hometown of Prague in 1911, Rilke calls himself a "rocket that has ended up in the bushes, huffing and puffing but to no one's enjoyment." In addition to "Rilke the rocket," there's Rilke—in his own words—"the sad and repugnant caterpillar," "the chrysalis in its cocoon," "the tree in winter without a single word-leaf," "the deaf mountain, quite rocky," "the photographic plate that's been exposed too long," "the student of life who is held back a grade for failing his classes." All of these slightly mocking self-descriptions allow Rilke to share wisdom while being neither preachy nor prophetic, yet still deeply poetic: regardless of what theme he is discussing, the poet reveals himself in these passages to be a sage of immanence.

Rilke's Aesthetics

Rilke's work constitutes a turning point and an anomaly in the tradition of modern poetry. He is at once a committed formalist, a master of the most intricate rhymes adapted to traditional poetic forms, and yet someone who responds explicitly to the social realities of alienation in a consumerist mass society. Much of Rilke's reputation and influence, especially among later poets, rests on his formalism. It is most often associated with *New Poems,* where one finds Rilke's exacting poetic renderings of animals, paintings, inanimate objects, and individuals that he observed at museums, during zoo visits, and in the city of Paris. The perplexing strength of Rilke's poetry, however, results from how this artful and self-consciously formal reflection on the proper representation of flamingos, say, becomes a consideration of how to look at and, ultimately, how to live one's life. "A flock of flamingos," you ask, "imparting life lessons?" That is precisely the point: virtually all of us have a rather tenuous relationship to flamingos, mostly from visits to the zoo where they are fed a special diet to keep their pale feathers from losing their pink. But Rilke shows us that neither our frail connection to these birds nor their peculiar ornamental and slightly artificial-seeming status in menageries should prompt our dismissal of them as something less significant than a woman losing her sight, or washing a corpse, or the nature of love (all other themes in *New Poems*). For Rilke, a poem's theme is nothing but a "pretext." His aperçus serve the ambitious and presumably prepolitical, or ethical, function of recovering what by the time we perceive it has been marginalized or domesticated or appropriated already by convention (for disdain, for entertainment, for consumption). Rilke insists that even the smallest or most banal thing might deserve our undivided attention.

But art is not unique in its recourse to a pretext. Rilke's words concern not only aspiring poets and admirers. At any moment we all take respite from the overwhelming nature and challenge of existence by turning to "the pretexts of life," which Rilke identified as the necessary effort to name and define things; to approach people with the crutch of titles and names; to play the games that reward us with recognition, money, even moments of happiness; or to break down and define our experiences as pleasure, pain, or joy. We often decide in advance how we will respond to something rather than wait for the experience to play itself out according to its proper speed.

> It is true that even happiness can sometimes serve as a pretext for initiating us into that which by its very nature surpasses us.

What "surpasses us by its very nature" is that dimension of life in which Rilke wishes to remain, prior to feeling happy or sad about it, prior to constructing philosophical systems or ideologies above it, prior to composing a poem about it. He wishes to remain in this dimension, however, not to denigrate life and its many pretexts and the games we play but to recall that at any moment we and these pretexts might be surpassed by our being. His purpose is to alert us to what we are already initiated into but tend to overlook or forget. The guide *to* life is also a reminder *of* life.

The celebrated formal refinement of Rilke, which quickly merges with the publicly known image of the elegant, impeccably dressed and faultlessly polite creature of his own mythologizing, is not a turning away from existential urgency but a way to approach that which is too large to be addressed head-on. Every single word on the flamingo's downy white and reddish hue in "The Flamingos" is as precisely aimed at expressing this richness of existence as Rilke's weighty contemplations in his letters on the nature of death, the ecstasies of love, or the fundamental innocence of sexual desire. Each intricately chiseled rhyme joins as effortlessly with the great roaring of existence as do the tender, profoundly affecting sentences of condolence in his correspondence. For Rilke, it is not merely a mistake to consider one aspect of life more important than another one and to elevate our memories of childhood or intimations of mortality, say, above the experience we might have upon encountering flamingos, a stray dog, or a hydrangea: it's an evasion. To celebrate Rilke for the refinement of his language alone is to fixate on the means of his poetry at the expense of its ends—to miss his urging that we be open to reality in all of its manifestations.

The interest of Rilke's letters lies with his willingness to account for what came his way without simply mastering it formally and instead to continually adapt his insights to that life that would be reliably represented only once it had been fundamentally understood. Rilke's letters, where he could try out language beyond his talents as a poet, are the reason why his ultimate achievements are far greater than anything one might have predicted from his first volumes of verse. He relinquished the safety of "reliable gain" and took the risk to develop his own idiom, even when he knew he could have continued to write good poetry in the manner for which he had already received accolades. The gift Rilke cultivated was not the ability to coax musicality out of all of language, to produce stunning rhymes and startlingly immediate images for abstract thought. Instead, it was his skill of receiving and processing reality anew each day without resting in the security of his talent and to write without the double safety harness of rhyme and formal structure.

The force of Rilke's letters results from his awareness that his life and "world," in a profound sense, surpassed and exceeded him. This is what constitutes life's richness for us all; it's also what can make it difficult. The reason the world "surpasses us" is because we make choices and form intentions that are wiped out simply by what happens; we take recourse to names and titles and seek happiness, but all of those forms of refuge may prove transient. Our ways of compartmentalizing the world and our failing to see with equanimity each of its aspects without preference, judgment, or distraction, Rilke writes on January 5, 1921, "puts us in the wrong, makes us culpable, kills us." And yet this fear of a gradual death brought about by our failure to be mindful—really a death of the imagination—reminds us that it is in fact not a question of mastering or subduing life but of living it. Rilke's sense of "culpability" allows him to formulate a vision of life that is more integrated than the way he actually lived; the force of his words results from the tension between this emphasis on acceptance and his equally strong preferences about the world around him.

Mindfulness in Rilke

Indisputably, in his life Rilke preferred to accept those aspects of reality that came with room service and a pleasant view. Alas, the biographical details are hard to ignore. The tension between Rilke's unshakable conviction in his "task," heroically shared by his steadfast, generous editor and magnanimous patrons, and his frequent illnesses, money trouble, and heartache make for a compelling biography. But the image of the poet outmatched by existence who will find in a stoic death the "quiet denied to him in life" is not only full of pathos; it's also a distortion since it neglects the fact that Rilke wrote throughout and often directly out of the difficult periods of his life.

We might as well debunk the version of Rilke the healer here. Rilke's work has been read as a defense against the brittleness of life under modern conditions. But when in 1908 his wife sent him a copy of *Speeches by Gotama Buddha,* translated from the Pali by the eminent German Indologist Karl Eugen Neumann, Rilke did not read it. The book had quickly become a bestseller and would

serve to introduce generations of readers, some already primed by
Arthur Schopenhauer's philosophy, to Eastern spiritual thought.
Thomas Mann cherished his three-volume copy and took it with
him on each transatlantic move, Edmund Husserl was inspired to
write an essay on Neumann's book, and Hermann Hesse drew on
it for much of his work. Rilke thanks his wife for sending the book
but explains that he will not be able to read it. "I opened [the
book] and already with the first words a shudder engulfed me . . .
[W]hy does this unfamiliar gesture of hesitation rise in me which
is so alienating to you?: It might be that I respond like this for the
sake of Malte Laurids [the hero of Rilke's novel] who I have put off
for a while already." The Buddha book is closed and forgotten—or,
if you will, repressed—after the initial shudder. Rilke then outlines
his belief that he must defend his own projects against all rivals for
his attention (among whom, it must be said, counts his wife). But
when Rilke writes that "a shudder engulfed him" upon opening
the book, it is also an uncanny shudder of recognition. Rilke
knows that his project is nothing else but to write his own Buddha
book; the aborted encounter with Gotama Buddha's speeches
prompts another bout of letter writing where he develops, in his
own language, all of the themes and terms for his impending work.
By developing his own understanding of life rather than adopting
a distant belief system, Rilke turns away from Buddha's words to-
ward his own work and ultimately comes closer to quasi-Buddhist
principles than fellow writers Mann, Husserl, and Hesse, who helped
popularize Eastern philosophies in the West.

Three years before this encounter with Buddha's words, Rilke
had lived for a while in a small house on the property of sculptor
Auguste Rodin in Meudon near Paris, surrounded by the great
artist's works and observing the daily practice of the man who em-

bodied his ideal of the pure artist. Looking out from his window, Rilke faced Rodin's massive sculpture *Buddha at Rest.* "After dinner I retreat quite soon to my little house, where I am by 8:30 at the latest. Then before me is the great blossoming night filled with stars, and below me in front of the window the pebble path rises to a small hill on which in fanatical speechlessness stands the likeness of a Buddha, dispensing the inexpressible unity of his gesture under all of the skies of day and night in silent reserve. 'C'est le centre du monde,' I said to Rodin." Rilke, who feels exceptionally happy during this stay in Rodin's world, recognizes himself in the Buddha figure. But instead of remaining in "fanatical speechlessness," Rilke will take from this "silent reserve" the strength to express the "inexpressible unity" of life and death, heaven and earth, himself and the other *in his own words.*

This way of communicating from the very center of his being, and thus without abandoning or moving away from it but by keeping it in "silent reserve," is the essence of Rilke's correspondence. He can both stay himself and yet give himself to others. In his poetry, he seeks to strike the perfect balance between a given object's interiority and the poet's and the reader's necessarily external consciousness. The process often involves a series of complex rhetorical reversals that obscure and ultimately efface any possible starting point, with the effect that the poem seems to begin at once strictly within its own images yet also in a reality it seeks to represent. In his letters, however, this complex exchange seems entirely natural and is easily followed by the reader: Rilke can expend and yet withhold himself, and the privacy afforded to him occasions the deepest intimacy.

By 1908 Rilke includes a total of three poems about Buddha in *New Poems.* These are probing poems, examining Rilke's faith in his capacity to enter into an object fully and grasp its position and true significance in his life, rather than just chronicling his emotional response to it. But Rilke would not accept another teacher. His "Buddha in Glory" is the final poem in *New Poems*. It begins with "Center of all centers, core of cores" and ends "Yet already there is begun inside of you / that which lasts beyond the suns."

In the very embodiment of an "inexpressible unity," which is for Rilke the apotheosis of the work of art, there is a magnificence that exceeds this unity. The completion of the Buddha's glory is a task Rilke set to accomplish in his poetry; his letters bear witness to this attempt. That is why he thanked his wife for the *Speeches of Gotama Buddha,* immediately shut the book, and continued writing his own guide to life that cannot be reduced to another's teachings, image, or text.

Rodin did not last as Rilke's teacher, ultimately showing the ambitious and needy poet the door rather than the path to enlightenment. Many of Rilke's poems in *New Poems* were written because Rodin had sent the young poet to the zoo where he was instructed to spend hours looking at the animals and to spend those same hours away from Rodin's studio, where the master needed to work unobserved for a while. Eventually, Rodin dismissed Rilke abruptly from the task of his assistant owing to a misunderstanding. (Rilke had signed his name to a letter addressed to one of Rodin's buyers with whom he had become friendly; Rodin erroneously assumed that Rilke was abusing his role as scribe to forge his own connections.) Rilke took the firing in stride and penned a remarkable letter the next morning to Rodin where he prophesied—correctly—that the two men would resume their friendship. In the brief letter, Rilke suggested to Rodin that although the reasons for firing Rilke were hurtful and wrong, Rodin had been right in doing so. He had removed the person who proved a momentary distraction from the "work" and unwittingly liberated Rilke from his unspoken dependency on the master. Precisely because it was painful and disappointing, Rilke was prompted to take the break seriously and recognize it as a challenge to become an artist in his own right.

Rilke was disappointed a second time when Rodin lost, in his eyes, his dignity by falling in love late in life with a far younger admirer. Even if Rodin ultimately disappointed Rilke, however, he triggered in Rilke an urgent desire to find out what it means to commit oneself to a meaningful pursuit. Rodin constituted for Rilke what Schopenhauer had been for Nietzsche and what Rilke has become for many: the unanticipated occasion through another's life or text, as Nietzsche put it in 1874, some thirty years before Rilke met Rodin, "to come to oneself out of the bewilderment in which one usually wanders as in a dark cloud." And like Nietzsche, who ultimately dropped Schopenhauer when he recognized that to face himself was the true challenge, Rilke also turned inward after his stay with Rodin.

W. H. Auden was not alone in mocking Rilke's cult of solitude. But Rilke did not fetishize the rewards of loneliness. When he describes the retreat into the self to follow paths that he did not know existed, he does not bring only welcome news. What he does do, however, is explain the human psyche in ways that are all but unrivaled in the history of ideas. Ultimately, all of these descriptions and analyses chart a way out of Rilke the person, the biography, the man, into what he describes in "Buddha in Glory" as "that which lasts beyond the suns." It's not nirvana—we have seen that Rilke never read the book on Buddha, despised organized religion, and stringently sought to develop his proper terms for that to which he wished to bear witness: life in all of its glory and magnificence and abundance and sheer horror and also the uncertain, wavering search for it. Take down every word of the "dictation of existence," without skipping even the tiniest "and" or "but," Rilke admonishes himself—which means that in one's actual search for meaning, as long as one diligently transcribes each step on this path, there might be already the key to discovering one's being. This "meaning of life" is spelled out already before our eyes and will not be supplied from elsewhere.

Rilke experienced the anonymity of everyday existence as a painful contraction of an individual's world. The more thinly a person is stretched across the grid of everyday life and the "richer" her life might seem, the less likely it is that she is at home within herself. And without being at home in oneself, even the most generous individual must shortchange everyone around her. When a close friend deplores her weakness in handling a series of personal challenges, Rilke counsels her with amazing psychological acuity and a typical dose of humility:

> You are wrong to think of yourself as "weak" . . . You have this impression because you are permanently stretched thin and every day find yourself poised to accommodate the hundreds of things that your life both gives and takes from you, without anything really staying there. This probably cannot be changed. But what can be changed is perhaps the constitution in which you accomplish these things (now I feel unbelievably immodest and pompous in writing this, I who barely do not even know how to take half a step in any direction . . .). I have often been alarmed that even something that *is* your most serious concern could assume the shape of a diversion—how should I put it: because it took its place in line with all the other diversions for fear of oth-

> erwise not receiving a turn at all . . . I know that there are times
> when it is basically a salvation to consider everything as a diver-
> sion, but these are exceptions, short periods, convalescences.

When life is taken as a diversion, it strangely becomes less than what it could be. What is important will then disguise itself as something entertaining, fun, and pleasant in order to get our attention. Fundamentally, life requires us to yield to its "velocity" if we want to partake of what it can offer. In a typical gesture, Rilke points out that such a stance toward life might call for exceptions and that he, for one, has not attained it. But tucked into this half-ironic aside might be the second lesson: there is no permanent stance that we might assume in life. We will always be at a loss about the next step when we allow ourselves to respond to life at its proper speed, without deciding in advance how fast or slow we want to take it. This is no different from Rilke's understanding of how poetry must approach every subject on its own terms and achieve a state where the subject's and the poet's different "velocities" coincide. Only then can it become apparent what the significance of a given object or person and place might be in our lives.

This is, then, not a philosophy of self-reliance and the admonition to "trust thyself" but a welcome to the ways in which you might surprise yourself and learn to relate to—and let go of—yourself in a less possessive spirit.

The Reception of Rilke

Of course, Rilke had been recognized as a major poet during his lifetime. He received stipends from the Austrian government and groups of donors, and some of his books sold relatively well. Because of his increasing need for anonymity, Rilke adopted the habit of refusing all official honors and awards. But because he sounded a new note in poetry and because this note penetrated even readers intoxicated by the shrill excitements of expressionist verse, prose, and theater exploding all over Europe at this time, there was also resistance. Already in the 1920s, Rilke's readers were disparaged as young girls and old maids. Rilke had made it a habit never to read criticism or reviews of his work. "Which does not mean," he clarified, "that I have not drawn joy and advantage from the warmth of an occasional personal agreement, or even someone disagreeing with my artistic aims as it finds expression in an intimate conversation. Such influences originate in life—and to resist them at any point I have never considered." Rilke broke his vow of silence only once with regard to an insinuation that he had betrayed the German language when he published a cycle of poems in French in 1925. He dismissed the charge as unfounded because "the German language had not been given to me as something alien; it works its effects out of me, it speaks out of my essence." The background to this attack on Rilke was the postwar occupation of Germany's industrial region of the Ruhr Valley by French troops to prevent Germany's rearmament, which many Germans deeply resented and which ultimately had disastrous political consequences. Rilke's poetry, filled with chrysanthemums and unicorns and written by a citizen of the erstwhile Austro-Hungarian monarchy born in Prague, had become the lightning rod for German, anti-French nationalist anxieties.

The second clouding of Rilke's stature occurred after 1968, when a new guard of professors in Germany rejected what they considered Rilke's apolitical cult of *Innerlichkeit,* or interiority. The revolution was not about to occur from within, argued these reformers of Germany's university system, and by the time the radicals had been granted tenure Rilke had been all but dropped from seminar reading lists. Not surprisingly, though, the poetry survived outside of the university's walls. When the new generation of scholars came to realize that revolutions—to which Rilke was not opposed on principle—are matters not only of the intellect but also of the body and the heart, they discovered that Rilke had continued to be read all along by the students whom they had been lecturing. But recent defenses of Rilke as a political thinker, such as an albeit well-intentioned six-hundred-page volume of his "letters on politics" published in Germany, similarly miss the mark. They try to politicize a poet who was highly doubtful about the strict distinction of the personal and the political. Rilke endures his contradictions, and even those remarks less suitable to our tastes and our time neither diminish nor augment what he writes elsewhere.

Through celebration and through censure, urgent attempts have been made to assign Rilke to a fixed state of poetic development and to delimit his reach by means of critical acclaim and public renown. The letters burst out of these classifications; they even shatter "the sum of misunderstandings that gather around a name," which Rilke defined as the nature of fame.

Translating Rilke

Among the most powerful letters are those in which Rilke expresses condolence. The idea for this book, indeed, was born when I was at a loss for words and couldn't find an appropriate poem to read at my father's funeral in Germany. I was unsure whether I could speak but also felt that this was a responsibility no one else could assume for me. The following passage from one of Rilke's letters seemed to put these feelings into words:

> It has seemed to me for a long time that the influence of a loved one's death on those he has left behind ought to be none other than that of a higher responsibility. Does the one who is passing away not leave a hundredfold of everything he had begun to be continued by those who survive him—if they had shared any kind of inner bond at all? Over the past few years I have been forced to gain intimate knowledge of so many close experiences of death. But with each individual who was taken from me, the tasks around me have only increased. The heaviness of this un-explained and possibly mightiest occurrence, which has assumed the reputation of being arbitrary and cruel only due to a misun-derstanding, presses us more deeply into life and demands the most extreme duties of our gradually increasing strengths.

I read these words in German at that occasion and then translated them and additional passages from German, and occasionally French, into English. I felt a distinct need to render available this side of Rilke to my English-speaking adult self as well. The movement from German into English also afforded me a way to relive and re-experience, now more consciously through the task of translation, my own first, joyous encounters with Rilke's words. Of equal im-portance was my gradual sense, put in its proper terms only by Rilke in a comment on his French poems written in a period he experienced as a second youth, that one always lives a "younger" existence than one's chronological age when one lives in a language that has been acquired later in life. Sometimes a second language may afford you the opportunity to reclaim through the act of trans-lation parts of your development that had passed you by in your own native language owing to that idiom's seeming transparency. My translations are guided by this sense of discovery and renewed appreciation for words and phrases that I was now able to claim for myself a second time, this time in English. The effort to render Rilke in English, rather than turn English into what Rilke might have sounded like in the language he did not master or enjoy, grows out of the experience of hearing Rilke open up German in ways that leave that language sounding less, well, German. My point was, above all, to re-create for English readers the experience of rhythm that is afforded to native German readers by Rilke's prose. This meant, however, finding a new rhythm that is properly suited to English rather than forcing English, in the name of literalism, into a teutonic frame and thus losing the grace of Rilke's words. In *The Notebooks of Malte Laurids Brigge,* Rilke advises that to write poetry one must wait for one's memories and experiences "to have changed into our very blood, into glance and gesture." The same applies for translation: the original must course for long periods through the translator's ears and mind and body, only to be cast often quite suddenly into the target language, at which point it adapts to and occasionally stretches the gestalt and rhythms of that idiom. And that idiom must be full of breath and life, which means that it might strain a bit against the syntax and sounds in which these sentences are now reborn. I don't share the belief held by some of Rilke's translators that German is more capable than English of expressing sustained thought. If such differences exist, they surely belong with individual speakers and not whole languages, and if there are differences between the ways one may structure an argument or describe an emotional state in a given tongue, these differences can be acknowledged but do not suggest the inherent superiority of any one language over another. In my case, translating Rilke quite unexpectedly gave language, for me now living in my "younger" English-speaking self, to one of life's pivotal and difficult experiences of passing into true adulthood.

On December 4, 1926, his fifty-first birthday, Rilke asked from his hospital bed for cards to be printed that were then to be mailed to far over a hundred active correspondents, all of them waiting for his word. The card read, in both German and French:

> Monsieur Rainer Maria Rilke, seriously ill, asks to be excused; he finds himself incapable of taking care of his correspondence. December 1926.

On December 29, 1926, Rilke is dead. The task of his correspondence had assumed absolute moral importance for the poet; his failure to live up to his correspondents' desire for his letters pained him deeply. But to ask his correspondents to forgive him for not writing means, in this poignant card, effectively to be excused for being "seriously ill" and thus, ultimately, to be excused for dying. Rilke knew his silence would disappoint, and by apologizing for it he recognized and finally assumed the role of counselor, confessor, spiritual adviser, and sage of the everyday that many of his correspondents had acknowledged and welcomed for years but that he had half-mockingly refused all along. The self-valediction by a man who pleaded with friends to keep a priest from his hospital bed at all costs and who was very reluctant to permit doctors access because he feared the division they created between his body and himself, is part of Rilke's legacy. "His correspondence" had become not just simply a task but a moral responsibility; it had attained the status usually accorded poetry. When Rilke asked for the card to be printed in both German and French, he also split himself into two languages and thus opened the possibility that either he had lost his notion of belonging to a native idiom or culture, or he recognized his voice to reach beyond what he had been identified with throughout his life. In this final written missive to the world, Rilke neither apologized nor voiced regret that he would write no more poetry; in the very act of crafting his correspondence, however, he had revealed a side of himself that could not be forgotten.

THE
POET'S
GUIDE TO
LIFE

Do not believe that the person who is trying to offer you solace lives his life effortlessly among the simple and quiet words that might occasionally comfort you. His life is filled with much hardship and sadness, and it remains far behind yours. But if it were otherwise, he could never have found these words.

[T]here are so many people who expect of me, I don't know exactly what—help, advice (of me who finds himself so baffled and helpless before life's most tremendous urgencies!)—and although I know that they are mistaken, that they are wrong in this regard, I am tempted nonetheless (and I don't believe that this is an act of vanity!) to share with them a few of my experiences—some of the fruits of my long solitudes . . . And women and young girls, terribly abandoned even at the bosom of their families—and newlyweds, horrified by what just happened to them . . . , and then all of these young people, for the most part revolutionary workers who leave the state prisons completely directionless and who stumble into "literature" by writing poems like mean drunks . . . : what to tell them? How to lift up their desperate heart, how to shape their disfigured will, which has assumed the character of something borrowed and altogether provisional under the impact of events and which they now carry inside themselves like an alien power that they hardly know how to use!

ON LIFE AND LIVING

*You Have to
Live Life to the Limit*

There is only a single, urgent task: to attach oneself someplace to nature, to that which is strong, striving and bright with unreserved readiness, and then to move forward in one's efforts without any calculation or guile, even when engaged in the most trivial and mundane activities. Each time we thus reach out with joy, each time we cast our view toward distances that have not yet been touched, we transform not only the present moment and the one following but also alter the past within us, weave it into the pattern of our existence, and dissolve the foreign body of pain whose exact composition we ultimately do not know. Just as we do not know how much vital energy this foreign body, once it has been thus dissolved, might impart to our bloodstream!

If we wish to be let in on the secrets of life, we must be mindful of two things: first, there is the great melody to which things and scents, feelings and past lives, dawns and dreams contribute in equal measure, and then there are the individual voices that complete and perfect this full chorus. And to establish the basis for a work of art, that is, for an image of life lived more deeply, lived more than life as it is lived today, and as the possibility that it remains throughout the ages, we have to adjust and set into their proper relation these two voices: the *one* belonging to a specific moment and the *other* to the group of people living in it.

Wishes! Desires! What does life know about them? Life urges and pushes forward and it has its mighty nature into which we stare with our waiting eyes.

•

Life takes pride in not appearing uncomplicated. If it relied on simplicity, it probably would not succeed in moving us to do all those things that we are not easily moved to do . . .

•

A conscious fate that is aware of our existence . . . yes, how often we long for such a fate that would make us stronger and affirm us. But would such a fate not instantly become a fate that beholds us from the outside, observes us like a spectator, a fate that we would no longer be alone with? The fact that we have been placed into a "blind fate" that we inhabit allows us to have our own perspective and is the very condition of our perspicacious innocence. It is due only to the "blindness" of our fate that we are so profoundly related to the world's wonderful density, which is to say to the totality that we cannot survey and that exceeds us.

•

Seeing is for us the most authentic possibility of acquiring something. If god had only made our hands to be like our eyes—so ready to grasp, so willing to relinquish all things—then we could truly acquire wealth. We do not acquire wealth by letting something remain and wilt in our hands but only by letting everything pass through their grasp as if through the festive gate of return and homecoming. Our hands ought not to be a coffin for us but a bed sheltering the twilight slumber and dreams of the things held there, out of whose depths their dearest secrets speak. Once out of our hands, however, things ought to move forward, now sturdy and strong, and we should keep nothing of them but the courageous morning melody that hovers and shimmers behind their fading steps.

For property is poverty and fear; only to have possessed something and to have let go of it means carefree ownership!

*

To look at something is such a wonderful thing of which we still know so little. When we look at something, we are turned completely toward the outside by this activity. But just when we are most turned toward the outside like that, things seem to take place within us that have longed for an unobserved moment, and while they unfold within us, whole and strangely anonymous, *without us,* their significance begins to take shape in the external object in the form of a strong, convincing, indeed their only possible name. And by means of this name we contentedly and respectfully recognize what is happening inside us without ourselves touching upon it. We understand it only quietly, entirely from a distance, under the sign of a thing that had just been alien and in the next instant is alienated from us again.

*

It does not happen frequently that something very great is condensed into a thing that can be held entirely in one hand, in one's own, impotent hand. Just as when one finds a tiny bird that is thirsty. You take it away from the edge of death, and the little heartbeats increase gradually in the warm, trembling hand like the wave at the edge of a giant ocean for which you are the shore. And you suddenly realize, while holding this little recovering animal, that life is recovering from death. And you hold it up. Generations of birds, and all of the forests over which they pass, and all of the skies into which they will rise. And is any of this easy? No: you are very strong to carry the heaviest burden in such an hour.

⁘

Each experience has its own velocity according to which it wants to be lived if it is to be new, profound, and fruitful. To have wisdom means to discover this velocity in each individual case.

⁘

Wishes are the memories coming from our future!

⁘

Be out of sync with your times for just one day, and you will see how much eternity you contain within you.

⁘

After all, life is not even close to being as logically consistent as our worries; it has many more unexpected ideas and many more facets than we do.

⁘

My god, how magnificent life is precisely owing to its unforeseeability and to the often so strangely certain steps of our blindness.

⁘

Life has been created quite truthfully in order to surprise us (where it does not terrify us altogether).

⁘

How numerous and manifold is everything that is yet to come, and how differently it all surfaces and how differently it all passes from the way we expect. How poor we are in imagination, fantasy, and expectation, how lightly and superficially we take ourselves in making plans, only for reality then to arrive and play its melodies on us.

•

The longer I live, the more urgent it seems to me to endure and transcribe the whole dictation of existence up to its end, for it might just be the case that only the very last sentence contains that small and possibly inconspicuous word through which everything we had struggled to learn and everything we had failed to understand will be transformed suddenly into magnificent sense. And who can be sure if in the realm of the beyond it might not somehow matter that here we had reached precisely *that end* that was ultimately meant for us. There is also no certainty that new challenges might not confront us on the other side while we flee from here completely exhausted—challenges that the soul, as it finds itself shaken and without having been either summoned or prepared, would face even more than other tasks with a sense of shame.

•

It is not possible to have an adequate image of how inexhaustible the expansiveness and possibilities of life are. No fate, no rejection, no hardship is entirely without prospects; somewhere the densest shrub can yield leaves, a flower, a fruit. And somewhere in god's furthest providence there surely exists already an insect that will gather riches from this flower or a hunger that will be sated by this fruit. And if this fruit is bitter it will have astonished at least one eye, and will have provided it pleasure and have triggered curiosity for the shapes and colors and crops of the shrub. And if the fruit were to fall, it would fall into the abundance of that which is yet to come. Even in its final decay it contributes to this future by turning it into more abundant, more colorful, and more urgent growth.

•

I have by now grown accustomed, to the degree that this is humanly possible, to grasp everything that we may encounter according to its particular intensity without worrying much about how long it will last. Ultimately, this may be the best and most direct way of expecting the *utmost* of everything—even its duration. If we allow an encounter with a given thing to be shaped by *this* expectation that it may last, every such experience will be spoiled and falsified, and ultimately it will be prevented from unfolding its most proper and authentic potential and fertility. All the things that cannot be gained through our pleading can be given to us only as something unexpected, something *extra:* this is why I am yet again confirmed in my belief that often nothing seems to matter in life but the longest patience.

•

Is not everything that happens to us, whether or not we desire or solicit it, always glorious and full of the purest, clearest justice?

•

What else does it mean to live but precisely this daring undertaking of filling a mold that one day will be broken off one's new shoulders, so that, now free in this new metamorphosis, one may become acquainted with all the other beings that have been magically transported into the same realm?

•

We lead our lives so poorly because we arrive in the present always unprepared, incapable, and too distracted for everything.

It is possible to feel so very much abandoned at times. And so much depends on the tiny indulgence of things, whether we can cope at all when they suddenly don't respond to us and don't move us along. Then we stand there inside the paltriness of our body, all alone—it is just like when we were children, when "they" were angry with us and pretended not to see us. Then the things were equally disloyal and there occurred a brief moment of *non*being that forced its way up to our heart and left room for nothing else. Suffering. For what is more *being* than precisely this heart, where the world alternates between becoming "object" and "self," inside and opposite, longing and fusion—and the beats of which coincide occasionally perhaps with, god knows, what infinite other measures in outer space . . . (perhaps by chance).

Finally—we know this—life's little wisdom is to wait (but to wait in the proper, pure state of mind), and the great grace that is bestowed on us in return is to survive . . .

How tremendous both life and death are as long as one does not incessantly consider both of them to be part of one greater whole while making hardly any distinctions between them. But *this* is precisely a task for angels and not our task, or rather ours only as an exception that might occur during moments that have been brought into existence slowly and painfully.

You have to live life to the limit, not according to each day but according to its depth. One does not have to do what comes next if

one feels a greater affinity with that which happens later, at a re-
move, even in a remote distance. One may dream while others are
saviors if these dreams are more real to oneself than reality and
more necessary than bread. In a word: *one ought to turn the most ex-
treme possibility inside oneself into the measure for one's life, for our life is
vast and can accommodate as much future as we are able to carry.*

●

Life has long since preempted every later possible impoverishment
through its astoundingly immeasurable riches. So what is there for
us to be afraid of? Only that this should be forgotten! But all
around us, within us, *how* many ways of helping us remember!

●

The following realization rivals in its significance a religion: that
once the background melody has been discovered one is no longer
baffled in one's speech and obscure in one's decisions. There is
a carefree security in the simple conviction that one is part of a
melody, which means that one legitimately occupies a specific space
and has a specific duty toward a vast work where the least counts as
much as the greatest. Not to be extraneous is the first condition for
an individual to consciously and quietly come into his own.

●

I want to thank you briefly for your letter; I can understand all of
it quite well and can even follow you into your sadness, into this
sadness that I know so deeply and which may of course be ex-
plained . . . And yet this sadness is nothing but a sensitive spot
within us, always the same spot, one of those that can no longer be
located once they begin to ache so that we fail to recognize and
treat it when we are numb with pain. I know all of this. There is a

kind of joy that is quite similar—and somehow we might have to get beyond both of them. I just recently thought that when I spent a few days climbing the steep mountains of Anacapri and was so filled with joy up there, so strenuously joyful in my soul. We let go of one or the other always yet again: this joyfulness and that sadness. We still do not *own* either of them. What do we amount to as long as we can get up and a wind, a gleam, a song wrought of the voices of a few birds in the air can seize us and do whatever it wants with us? It is good to hear all of this and to see it and to seize it, not to become numb toward it but on the contrary: everything is to be felt in countless ways in all its variations yet without losing ourselves to it. I once said to Rodin on an April day filled with spring: "How this [springtime] dissolves us and how we have to contribute to it with our own juices and make an effort to the point of exhaustion—don't you also know this?" And he, who surely knew on his own how to seize spring, with a quick glance: "Ah—I have never paid attention to that." That is what we have to learn: *not* to pay attention to certain things, to be *too* concentrated to touch in some sensitive spot the things that can never be reached with one's entire being, to feel everything only with *all* of life—then much (that is too narrow) will be excluded but everything important will take place . . .

.

Life is so very *true,* when taken in its entirety, that even the lie (if it does not emanate from base motives) gloriously shares in this unwavering truth.

.

Life goes on, and it goes past a lot of people in a distance, and around those who wait it makes a detour.

•

Do not believe that everything strong and beautiful will end up as something "ugly and ordinary," as you put it at this moment of inner turmoil—it *cannot* end this way because it does not end at all if it was something strong and beautiful. It continues to work its effects in unceasing transformations; it is only that these transformations frequently so vastly exceed our capacity to grasp and endure them. Frequently, when we are frozen by an event or if an event sheds its leaves and petals in front of our eyes in some other violent way, we dig up the soil around it in horror and shrink back from the ugliness of its roots where *that* which looks to us like transience lives. We have such a limited capacity to be just toward *all* phenomena and we are so quick to call ugly, as if turning spitefully and vengefully against ourselves, anything that simply does not correspond to the notion of beauty to which we subscribe at that moment. This is often nothing more than a—though often nearly intolerable—shifting of our attention; the clustered appearances of life are still so terribly disconnected and incompatible for our perception. Take a walk in the woods on a spring day. It's enough for us to allow our gaze to wander briefly into another category of existence to be facing destruction and disintegration rather than to be looking at life, and to perceive instead of joy, desolation; to feel instead of harmonious vibrations petrified, even exiled, from any insight and participation and commonality. But *what* does this say against spring? *What* against the forest? What against *us*? What, finally, against our possibilities to relate to and to recognize each other? Wherever our attention is thus redirected in our soul, in our interiority, it is of course all the more assaulting and disturbing— but one would call this shift "ugly and common" only if one recognized it as nothing but a conventional disillusionment or disappointment and not as the task to grasp an unceasingly particular, unique and incomparable metamorphosis in all of its peculiar reality.

·

Wherever we expect something great, it is of course not this or that particular thing that we expect, and it is altogether impossible to count on and expect anything at all since what is at stake is the unexpected, the unforeseen. There is no one less puzzled by the slowness of this process since the experience of my days is measured according to the great intervals of artistic growth.

·

How peculiar, the way life works. If this were not a bit arrogant, one would like to position oneself outside of it all, on the opposite side of everything *that happens* just in order not to miss anything at all—even there one would still remain rooted in life's true center, maybe there even more so than elsewhere, there where all things come together without having a proper name. But ultimately we are also quite attracted and taken in by names, by titles, by the pretexts of life, because the whole is too infinite and we recover from it only by naming it for a while with the name of *one* love, no matter how much this passionate delimitation then puts us in the wrong, makes us culpable, murders us . . .

·

Ah, we count the years and introduce divisions here and there and stop and begin anew and waver between these options. But everything that we encounter is so very much of one piece, and so intimately related to everything else, and has given birth to itself, grows, and is then raised so much to come into its own, that we basically just need *to be there,* if only unassumingly, if only authentically, the way the earth is there in its affirmation of the seasons, light and dark and wholly in space, longing to be supported by nothing but that web of influences and forces where the stars feel secure.

•

We make our way through Everything like thread passing through fabric: giving shape to images that we ourselves do not know.

•

Even the past is still a being in the fullness of its occurrence, if only it is understood not according to its content but by means of its intensity, and we—members of a world that generates movement upon movement, force upon force, and seems to cascade inexorably into less and less visible things—we are forced to rely upon the past's superior visibility if we want to gain an image of the now muted magnificence that still surrounds us today.

•

It is, after all, *one* strength within the human with which we achieve everything, a single steadfastness and pure direction of the heart. Whoever possesses that strength ought not to lose himself to fear.

•

How is it possible to live since the elements of this life remain entirely beyond our grasp? If we are continually inadequate in love, insecure in making decisions, and incapable in our relation to death, how is it possible to exist? I did not succeed in this book [*The Notebooks of Malte Laurids Brigge*], although it was born out of deepest inner commitment, to put into words my complete amazement at the fact that human beings have dealt for millennia with life (not even to mention with god) and still face so ineffectually these basic, most immediate, and, in truth, mere tasks (for what else is there to do today and for how much longer?) like so many baffled novices caught between terror and evasion. Is this not incomprehensible? Every time I allow myself to be astonished by this fact I feel myself entering a state of the highest consternation and even a kind of horror, but behind this horror there is something familiar, intimate, and of such intensity that my feelings fail me in deciding whether it is burning hot or icy cold.

·

It is possible that our nature indeed often takes revenge on us for the inappropriateness and foreignness of what we ask of it, and that between us and our surroundings there run cracks that remain not wholly on the surface. But why did our forebears read about all of those foreign things: by letting these things grow inside them into dreams, wishes, and vague fantastic images, by tolerating that, their heart changed gears, spurred on by some adventurousness or other; when standing at the window with boundless and misunderstood distance inside them and with a gaze that turned its back almost contemptuously on the courtyard and garden out there, they effectively conjured up all of *that which* we now have to deal with and basically make up for. When they lost sight of their surroundings, which they no longer perceived, they lost sight of all of reality. What was nearby seemed boring and mundane and what was far depended entirely on their mood and imagination. And closeness and distance were forgotten in this way. This is how it became our task not even to decide between proximity and distance, but to assume both and to reunite them as the one reality, which in truth has no divisions or closure and which is not common when it is nearby, but romantic when it is a bit further off, and not boring right here and over there quite entertaining. They were so terribly intent on distinguishing between what was strange and what was common back then; they did not notice how much of each is everywhere most densely intertwined. They saw only that whatever was near did not belong to them, and so they thought that anything of value that can actually be owned they would find abroad, and they longed for it. And their intense and inventive longing seemed proof to them of its beauty and greatness. For they still held on to the view that it is possible for us to take something into ourselves, draw it in and swallow it, while in fact we are so filled up from the beginning that not the tiniest thing could be added. Yet everything can have an effect on us. And all things affect us from a distance, the near as well as the remote things, nothing touches us; everything reaches us across divisions. And just as the most remote stars cannot enter us, the ring on my hand cannot do so either: everything that reaches us can do so only the way a magnet summons and aligns the forces in some susceptible object; in this way, all things can effect a new alignment within us. And in view of this insight, do proximity and distance not simply vanish? And is not this *our* insight?

I believe that one is never more just than at those moments when one admires unreservedly and with absolute devotion. It is in this spirit of unchecked admiration that the few great individuals whom our time was unable to stifle ought to be presented, precisely because our age has become so very good at assuming a critical stance.

Something is true only next to something else, and I always think the world has been conceived of with sufficient space to encompass everything: that which has been does not need to be cleared from its spot but only needs to be gradually transformed, just as whatever is yet to occur does not fall from the skies at the last moment but resides always already right next to us, around us and within our heart, waiting for the cue that will summon it to visibility.

It seems to me that the only way one can be helpful is to extend one's hand to someone else *involuntarily,* and without ever knowing how useful this will be. If love becomes all it can be through willpower, willpower can achieve even more when one wants to help. But the gods alone can procure help, and when they make use of us to accomplish their acts of charity they like to plunge us into impenetrable anonymity.

Even on days when fate wishes to bestow boundless gifts on them, most people make mistakes in accepting: they don't accept straightforwardly and consequently lose something while doing so, they take with a secondary purpose in mind, or they accept what is given to them as if they were being compensated for something else.

And yet life *is* transformation: all that is good is transformation and all that is bad as well. For this reason *he* is in the right who encounters everything as something that will not return. It does not matter whether he then forgets or remembers, as long as he had been fully present only for its duration and been the site, the atmosphere, the world for what happened, as long as it happened *within* him, in his center, whatever is good and what is bad—then he really has nothing else to fear because something else of renewed significance is always about to happen next. The possibility of intensifying things so that they reveal their essence depends so much on our participation. When things sense our avid interest, they pull themselves together without delay and are all that they can be, and in everything new the old is then whole, only different and vastly heightened.

.

We of the here and now are not satisfied for one moment in the time-world nor attached to it; we constantly exceed it and pass over to earlier ones, to our origins, and to those that seem to come after us. In that greatest *"open"* world everyone *is* not exactly "contemporary" precisely since the disappearance of time causes them all *to be.* Transience everywhere plunges into a deep being. And thus all the forms found here are to be used not only within temporal limits but as far as possible to be placed by us into those superior realms of significance in which we participate. But *not in a Christian sense* (from which I distance myself with increasing fervor) and instead in a purely earthly, deeply earthly, blissfully earthly consciousness it is our task to place what we see and touch *here* into the wider and widest context. Not into a beyond whose shadow darkens the earth but into a whole, into *the whole.* Nature and all of the objects of our daily use are preliminary and frail; as long as we are here, however, they are *our* possession and our friendship, accessories to our suffering and joy, just as they had been the intimates of our predecessors. It is thus our task not only not to malign and take down everything that is here but rather, because of the transience which we have in common with it, to comprehend and transform with an innermost consciousness these appearances and things. Transform? Yes, for it is our task to impress this provisional, transient earth upon ourselves so deeply, so agonizingly, and so passionately that its essence rises up again "invisibly" within us. *We are the bees of the invisible. We ceaselessly gather the honey of the visible to store it in the great golden hive of the Invisible.*

How good life is. How fair, how incorruptible, how impossible to deceive: not even by strength, not even by willpower, and not even by courage. How everything remains what it is and has only this choice: to come true, or to exaggerate and push too far . . .

All of our insights occur after the fact.

I basically do not believe that it matters to be happy in the sense in which people expect to be happy. But I can so absolutely understand the kind of arduous happiness that consists in rousing forces through a determined effort, forces that then start to work upon one's self.

History is not *all* of humanity but only an index of the water levels, of the low tides and floods; it is not the rushing water itself, nor the current nor the river's bed. The surges and destructions by which men are occupied, impassioned, elevated, and annihilated can be nothing but an allegory, like a retracing and vanishing of invisible architectures that constitute the true world-shape of our existence.

In life, in all of its forms, the static principle, which is our ultimate concern, has been realized: the principle that does not consist in establishing ourselves continually anew in instability but in coming to rest in the center to which we return from each risk and change. There you rest like a die in a cup. Surely, an unknown gambler's hand shakes the cup, casts you out, and out there you count upon landing either for a lot or very little. But after the die has been cast, you are put back into the cup and there, inside, in the cup, no matter *how* you come to lie, you signify all of its numbers, all of its sides. And there, inside the cup, luck or misfortune are of no concern, but only bare existence, being a die, having six sides, six chances, always again all of them—along with the peculiar certainty of not being able to cast oneself out on one's own and the pride in knowing that it takes a divine wager for anyone to be rolled from deep within this cup onto the table of the world and into the game of fate. This is the actual meaning of *A Thousand and One Nights* and the root of its suspense for those listening to these stories: that the porter, the beggar, the herder of camels—anyone who was cast without adding up to much—is scooped back into the cup to be wagered once more. And that it is the world into which one tumbles, among stars, to girls, children, dogs, and garbage; that there is nothing unclear about the circumstances into which one may fall. There might be something too great or too evil, too deceptive or plainly doomed there . . . but one is dealing either with other dice or with the throws and ghosts that shake the cups and wager their own stake in doing so. It is an honest game, unpredictable, and always begun anew, beyond one and yet played in a way that no one is ever worthless even for an instant, or bad, or shameful: for who can be responsible for falling this way or that out of the cup?

•

How old one would have to become to have truly admired enough and not to lag behind with regard to anything in the world. There is still so much that one underestimates, overlooks, and misrecognizes. God, how many opportunities and examples that invite us to become something—and in response to those, how much sluggishness, distractedness, and half-will on our side.

What we all need most urgently now: to realize that transience is not separation—for we, transient as we are, have it in common with those who have passed from us, and they and we exist together in one *being* where separation is just as unthinkable. Could we otherwise understand such poems if they had been nothing but the utterance of someone who was going to be dead in the future? Don't such poems continually address inside of us, in addition to what is found there now, also something unlimited and unrecognizable? I do not think that the spirit can make itself anywhere so small that it would concern only our temporal existence and our here and now: where it surges toward us there we are the dead and the living all at once.

I believe in old age; to work and to grow old: this is what life expects of us. And then one day *to be old* and still be quite far from understanding everything—no, but to begin, but to love, but to suspect, but to be connected to what is remote and inexpressible, all the way up into the stars.

How wonderful to grow old when one has worked on life like a true craftsman; then there are no memories left that have not become thing, then there is nothing that has passed away: everything

is there, real, ravishingly real, it is there and *is* and has been ac-
knowledged by and entered into something greater, and it is linked
to the most remote past and impregnated with future.

.

Is it not peculiar that nearly all of the great philosophers and psy-
chologists have always paid attention to the earth and nothing but
the earth? Would it not be more sublime to lift our eyes from this
crumb, and instead of considering a speck of dust in the universe,
to turn our attention to space itself? Just imagine how small and in-
significant all earthly toils would suddenly appear at the moment
when our earth would shrink to the tiniest, swirling, aimless parti-
cle of an infinite world! And how the human being would have to
grow in size on his "small earth"!

Peculiar. Each bird that builds its home under the roof beams
first examines the spot it has chosen and over which a minuscule
part of its life shall now be dispersed. And the human being, mean-
while, is entirely satisfied with approximately and scarcely knowing
the earth and leaves the wide worlds above to waver and to change
their ways. Does it not seem as if we are still positioned quite low
since our gaze is so consistently fixed on the ground?

.

We have to be committed not to miss or neglect any opportunity
to suffer, to have an experience, or to be happy; our soul arises re-
freshed from all of that. It has a resting place at those heights that
are difficult to reach, and it is at home where one can advance no
further: up there we have to carry it. But as soon as we put it down
for dead at those extreme spots it awakens and takes flight into skies
and celestial depths that from now on belong to us.

.

I confess that I consider life to be a thing of the most untouchable deliciousness, and that even the confluence of so many disasters and deprivations, the exposure of countless fates, everything that insurmountably increased for us over the past few years to become a still rising terror cannot distract me from the fullness and goodness of existence that is inclined toward us. There would be little sense in approaching you with good wishes if each wish were not *preceded* by this conviction that the goods of life arise pure, undamaged, and, at their very bottom, desirable out of upheaval and ruin.

On Being with Others

Others

To Be a Part,

That Is Fulfillment for Us

To be a part, that is fulfillment for us: to be integrated with our
solitude into a state that can be shared.

.

All disagreement and misunderstanding originate in the fact that
people search for commonality *within* themselves instead of search-
ing for it in the things *behind* them, in the light, in the landscape, in
beginning and in death. By so doing they lose themselves and gain
nothing in turn.

.

Injustice has always been a part of human movements; it is inher-
ent to them. If one knows a way into the future one must not lose
time by avoiding injustices; one simply has to overcome them
through action.

.

This is one of the most unconditional tasks of friendship: to be
pure in every No, wherever one is not absolutely flooded with the
most infinite Yes.

.

If one could only look back at every human countenance that had
even just once seriously and openly turned toward us, without any
self-reproach for having betrayed or overlooked it. But one lives in
the density of one's own body, which imposes its particular mea-
sure already in purely physical terms (because after all there is noth-
ing to go on but this physical I), and since one lives, I think, in the
awkwardness of this body and confined and imprisoned by the sur-

rounding world in which one moves . . . one is not always as free, as loving, and as innocent as one should be able to be according to one's proper resources and convictions. And frequently insecurity and distractedness limit us further. What bighearted confidence in oneself would be needed to respond to every voice that reaches us with the truest sense of hearing and the most undistracted reply.

•

But there is something that I do not grasp. Do you know it? How as a young person, as a young girl, can one go off in order to take care of unknown, sick people? I very much would like to admire such behavior, and I have the sense that one cannot admire it nearly enough. But something in this conviction bothers me. I am concerned that our times are responsible for such disproportionate decisions. Is there not something in them that dissolves for many generous and strong intentions their natural point of application? You should imagine that this touches me quite in the same way as the fact that all the greatest paintings and art objects are now in museums where they no longer belong to anyone. Of course, we are told: This is where they belong to everyone. But I cannot get used to this commonality at all; I never manage to believe in it. Are all of the most valuable things truly meant to end up in this commonality? This seems to me, and here I cannot help myself, as if one opened a small flask of rose oil outside and there left it uncorked: surely its strength is now somewhere in the open air but so dispersed and spread out that this most intense of all scents must now be considered lost for our senses. I am not sure if you recognize what I mean.

•

Before a human being thinks of others he must have been unapologetically himself; he must have taken the measure of his nature in order to master it and employ it for the benefit of others like himself.

•

And yet, and yet: how hopeful each individual person is every time again, how real, how well intentioned, how rich. When one then looks at the confused and dreary crowd, it is impossible to grasp that the individual loses himself there in this way as if without a trace.

•

As soon as two people have resolved to give up their togetherness, the resulting pain with its heaviness or particularity is already so completely part of the life of each individual that the other has to sternly deny himself to become sentimental and feel pity. The beginning of the agreed-upon separation is marked precisely by this pain, and its first challenge will be that *this pain already* belongs separately to each of the two individuals. This pain is an essential condition of what the now solitary and most lonely individual will have to create in the future out of his reclaimed life.

If two people managed not to get stuck in hatred during their honest struggles with each other, that is, in the edges of their passion that became ragged and sharp when it cooled and set, if they could stay fluid, active, flexible, and changeable in all of their interactions and relations, and, in a word, if a mutually human and friendly consideration remained available to them, then their decision to separate cannot easily conjure disaster and terror.

•

When it is a matter of a separation, pain should already belong in its entirety to that other life from which you wish to separate. Otherwise the two individuals will continually become soft toward each other, causing helpless and unproductive suffering. In the process of a firmly agreed-upon separation, however, the pain itself constitutes an important investment in the renewal and fresh start that is to be achieved on both sides. People in your situation might have to communicate as friends. But then these two separated lives should remain *without* any knowledge of the other for a period and exist as far apart and as detached from the other as possible. This is necessary for each life to base itself firmly on its new requirements and circumstances. Any subsequent contact (which may then be truly new and perhaps very happy) has to remain a matter of unpredictable design and direction.

If you find that you scare yourself upon recognizing that you become unbridled and terrifying and even a torment for the other person whom you have conquered in love, then you might wish to conjure a mental counterimage showing that the conquest and ownership of another human being—so that one could use this person then for one's own (often so fatefully conditioned) pleasure— that the use of another human being does not exist, must not exist, cannot exist—and you will regain the distance and awe that will compel you to adjust your excitement according to the measures established during your courtship. It happens frequently that the kind of happiness such as that experienced by you in loving and being loved unleashes not only new forces in a young man but uncovers entirely different, deeper layers of his nature from which then the most uncanny findings erupt overwhelmingly: but our confusions have always been part of our riches, and where their violence scares us we are simply startled by the unfathomed possibilities and tensions of our strength—and this chaos, as soon as we gain some distance from it, immediately triggers within us the premonition of new orders and, if we can enlist our courage in such premonitions even just a bit, the curiosity and desire to achieve this unforeseeable future order! I have written "distance"; should there be anything like advice that I would be able to suggest to you, it would be the hunch that you need to search for *that* now, for distance. Distance: from the current consternation and from those new conditions and proliferations of your soul that you enjoyed back at the time of their occurrence but of which you have until now not at all truly taken possession. A short isolation and separation of a few weeks, a period of reflection, and a new focusing of your crowded and unbridled nature would offer the greatest probability of rescuing all of that which seems in the process of destroying itself in and through itself.

•

Nothing locks people in error as much as the daily repetition of error—and how many individuals that ultimately became bound to each other in a frozen fate could have secured for themselves, by means of a few small, pure separations, that rhythm through which the mysterious mobility of their hearts would have inexhaustibly persisted in the deep proximity of their interior world-space, through every alteration and change.

•

Marriage is difficult, and those who take it seriously are beginners who suffer and learn!

•

I am of the opinion that "marriage" as such does not deserve as much emphasis as it has accrued because of the conventional development of its nature. No one would dream of expecting a single individual to be "happy"—once someone is married, however, everyone is very astonished when he is *not* happy! (Meanwhile it actually isn't all that important to be happy, neither as an individual nor as a married person.) In some regards, marriage simplifies the conditions of life, and such a union surely augments the strengths and determinations of two young people so that they jointly seem to reach further into the future than before. Only these are sensations by which one cannot live. Above all marriage is a new task and a new seriousness—a new challenge and a question regarding the strength and kindness of each participant and a new great danger for both.

In marriage, the point is not to achieve a rapid union by tearing down and toppling all boundaries. Rather, in a good marriage each person appoints the other to be the guardian of his solitude and thus shows him the greatest faith he can bestow. The *being-together* of two human beings is an impossibility; where it nonetheless seems to be present it is a limitation, a mutual agreement that robs one or both parts of their fullest freedom and development. Yet once it is recognized that even among the *closest* people there remain infinite distances, a wonderful coexistence can develop once they succeed in loving the vastness between them that affords them the possibility of seeing each other in their full gestalt before a vast sky!

For this reason the following has to be the measure for one's rejection or choice: whether one wishes to stand guard at another person's solitude and whether one is inclined to position this same person at the gates of one's own depth of whose existence he learns only through what issues forth from this great darkness, clad in festive garb.

There is no general response to your husband's question as posed in your letter. Only the most *personal* solution for each individual case will make clear whether or not an individual does damage to himself by sacrificing something for someone else. Even the seeming renunciation of one's own ideals out of one's solicitude for another does not have to be a final renunciation but can become an opportunity. An individual who makes a strong effort on behalf of someone else in a great gesture of subjugation might yet encourage within the other person *that* which he neglects in himself. And for some it might even appear more beautiful and rewarding to come to bloom in a beloved or in a greatly conceived commonality rather than in their own being.

Ultimately, this is what constitutes the events and values in the world: that time and again one hears of someone who has said things that one had thought only obscurely and who has done things that one had expressed only at a fortuitous moment. Such things make you grow. This awareness of conduits and lines reaching from distant solitary figures to us and from us to god knows where and to whom, this I consider our best feeling: it leaves us alone and yet simultaneously patches us into a great communality where we take hold and have help and hope.

When two or three people get together they are still not linked in any way. They are like string puppets whose wires rest in separate hands. It is not until *one* hand guides them all that they are enveloped by a commonality that forces them either to bow or to punch each other. And a human being's strengths are even there where his wires come to end in a hand that holds and governs them.

We are so rarely in a position to help. For this reason one must be absolutely focused wherever the faintest opportunity to do so arises.

*

To be able to help always also means to help oneself in some way!

*

In a world that attempts to dissolve divinity into a kind of anonymity, it had to happen that there developed a humanitarian misunderstanding that expects of human help what it cannot provide. And since divine kindness is so indescribably tied to divine firmness, an era that takes it upon itself to distribute kindness, thus preempting providence, unleashes at the same moment the most ancient stores of cruelty among men.

*

No book, just as no word of encouragement, may achieve anything decisive if the *person* who encounters it had not been prepared by something quite unintentional for a more profound reception and conception; if his hour of reflection and taking stock had not arrived in any case. In order to shift *that* hour into the center of his consciousness, one thing or another may then suffice: sometimes a book or an artistic object, sometimes a child's gaze, the voice of another person or a bird, and even sometimes a sound made by the wind, a creaking of the floor, or, when people were still spending time in front of an open fireplace (which I have been able to do on occasion), a gaze into the transformations of the flames. All this and even far smaller, seemingly coincidental things can trigger and affirm one's self-discovery or self-rediscovery. And at times even poets may be among those good occasions.

*

Our emotions cannot do anything but become greater through empathy. From empathy to imitation it is yet a different path— in a sense a backtracking. Empathy is directed toward the inside, whereas imitation leads back outside into visibility. As such, it is actually the immediate loss of that which can be claimed through the emotion of empathy. But in the direction toward the inside followed by empathy, of this I am sure, one cannot go too far. The further one ventures there, the more dependably one will tap into a previously unknown vein of one's own feelings. I consider imitators mostly to be individuals who did not muster enough empathy and who instead turned around halfway and by tracing their own footprints reached the outside again. Any engagement with a work of art would be absolutely hopeless without an empathic response that would lead almost to one's own annihilation but ultimately returns us to ourselves richer, stronger, and more capable of feeling. Empathy is humility, imitation is vanity—and thus it ought to be possible soon to notice whether one intends one or the other.

Perhaps the poet is intended to act truly outside of fate and becomes ambiguous, imprecise, untenable wherever he engages in it. Just as the hero becomes true only inside of his fate, the poet grows mendacious in it; the former maintains himself in tradition, the latter in indiscretion.

To be close to another person who holds *opposing* views while being a deep, committed friend can be a wonderful, shaping influence. For as long as one remains forced to consider (as one is primarily in one's relation to one's parents and other older people) anything other as something false, bad, hostile instead of plainly other, one will not enter into an unforced and just relation with the world where all things are meant to have a place: part and counter-part; I and the one who is most different from me. And only when such a complete world is admitted to and considered possible will one succeed in arranging one's own interiority with its internal contrasts and contradictions generously, spaciously, and with suffi-cient air to breathe.

There is a single, deadly mistake that we can make: to attach our-selves to another human being even if only for an instant.

From one human being to another everything is so difficult and so unrehearsed and so without a model and example that one would have to live within every relationship with complete attentiveness and be creative in every moment that requires something new and poses tasks and questions and demands . . .

It seems to me to result in nothing but disorder when a collective presumes that its efforts (an illusion, incidentally!) may relieve or abolish difficulties schematically. This might impair a person's free-dom much more than suffering itself, which imparts to the indi-vidual who confides in it indescribably fitting and almost tender instructions on how to escape it—if not to the outside, then to the inside. The wish to improve another person's situation presupposes a level of insight into his conditions that even a poet does not pos-sess with regard to a character he himself invented. A person trying to help is even less equipped to do so; his distractedness reaches completion with his gift. The wish to alter and improve another person's situation means to offer him in lieu of the difficulties in which he has practice and experience other difficulties that might find him even more baffled.

 .

Ultimately nobody can help anyone else in life; one has this recurring experience in every conflict and confusion: that one is alone.

This is not as bad as it may appear at first glance; it is also the best thing about life that everyone contains everything within himself: his fate, his future, his entire scope and world. Now there surely exist moments when it is difficult to be within oneself and to endure within one's own I. It happens that precisely when one ought to hold on to oneself more tightly and—one would almost have to say—more obstinately than ever, one attaches oneself to something external, and that during important events one shifts one's proper center out of oneself into something alien, into another human being. This is against the most basic principles of equilibrium and can lead to nothing but great difficulty.

 .

The privilege to cause joy is given to us far less frequently than one would think, partly owing to our often rigid incapacity to receive and partly owing to the imprecision and vagueness between people (this may always have been an obstacle), which has increased even more in confusing times. After all, even the most appropriate gift still requires the receiver to accommodate himself to an extreme degree. In cases of "well-matched" giving, in contrast, even this effort belongs to the natural movement of the person who receives the gift.

 .

Departures create a burden within our emotions. The distance stays behind them with greater emphasis and works and grows and gains hold of all the commonalities that ought to remain instinctive even for those who are very far apart . . .

•

How telling that some people have defined the human to be the common element and the site where everybody can find and recognize each other. One has to learn to realize that it is precisely the human that makes us lonely.

•

The more human we become, the more different we become. It is as if suddenly human beings would multiply a thousandfold. A collective name that used to be sufficient for thousands will soon be too narrow for ten human beings, and we will be forced to consider each individual entirely on his own. Just think: when at some point we will have human beings instead of populations, nations, families, and societies; when it will no longer be possible to group even three people under *one* name! Will the world not have to grow larger then?

•

We have all known for a long time that only purely honest and joyous attempts are possible from one individual to another, and that even the most wonderful success does not obey any internal rhythm, and that it does not even have any measure at all. And don't we also know that the capacities of a life can be tested only within that life, so that every being-cast-back-on-oneself has to be a natural occurrence, something necessary? To become superfluous somewhere means to need only yourself: if you are asked to achieve an ending somehow, this also means that you are receiving an order to begin anew; a new beginning is always possible—who should refuse it?

ON WORK

*Get Up Cheerfully on Days
You Have to Work*

Perhaps creating something is nothing but an act of profound remembrance.

·

Ah, this longing to be able to begin, and always all of these blocked paths. How will it be with my work? Every morning I get up for this useless and anxious waiting, and go to sleep disappointed, disoriented, and overcome with my inability. Ah, if I had a manual craft, a daily task, something closer . . . instead of this waiting for faraway things. Is it arrogance? Alas, for whom the will wavers, for him wavers the world.

·

This is the one experience that has been confirmed repeatedly and to which I have progressed slowly after a fearful, despondent childhood: that the true advances of my life could not be brought about by force but occur silently, and that I prepare for them while working quietly and with concentration on the things that on a deep level I recognize to be my tasks.

·

We have to mix our work with ourselves at such a deep level that workdays turn into holidays all by themselves, into our actual holidays.

·

Before they had a genuine opportunity to truly get to know work, people had already invented leisure as a diversion from and the opposite of false work. If they had waited, alas, and if they had been patient for a good while, then true work would have been slightly more within their reach and they would have realized that work cannot have an opposite just as the world cannot have one, or god, or any living soul. For *it is everything,* and what *it is not* is nothing and nowhere.

·

Get up cheerfully on days you have to work, if you can. And if you can't, what keeps you from doing so? Is there something heavy that blocks the way? What do you have against heaviness and difficulty? That it can kill you. So it is powerful and strong. This much you know about it. And what do you know about things that are light and easy? Nothing. We have no memory whatsoever of that which was easy and light. So even if you could choose, ought you not actually choose what is difficult? Don't you feel how it is related to you? . . . And are you not in agreement with nature when you make this choice? Don't you think a little sapling would have an easier time by staying in the soil? Things that are light and things that are heavy don't actually exist. Life itself is heavy and difficult. And you do actually want to live? Then you are mistaken in calling it your *duty* to take on difficulties. It's your survival instinct that pushes you to do it. So what is duty, then? It is duty to love what is difficult . . . You have to be there when it needs you.

·

What one writes as a very young person is of no significance whatsoever, just as what else one embarks on has almost no significance. Even the apparently most useless diversions can be a pretext for an inner focusing; one's nature might even instinctively seize such activities to turn the controlling observation and attention of a curious intellect away from those mental processes that wish to remain unrecognized. One may do *anything:* only this corresponds to the full scope of life. But one ought to be certain that nothing is done out of opposition, to defy obstructing circumstances, while thinking of others, or based on some kind of ambition. You must be certain that you are acting out of pleasure, strength, courage, or a sheer sense of abandon: that you *have to* act this way.

·

In the boundless heavens of work we are afforded one form of bliss that surpasses all others: that something first experienced much earlier is returned to us and can now be grasped and assimilated into the self with the love that has in the meantime grown more just. That is when our divisions begin to be adjusted, when something from the past returns as if from the future; something accomplished as something yet to be completed. And this is the first experience that positions us, out of sequence, at that spot in our heart that is in space and always equidistant from everything and subject to rising and to setting because of the unceasing movement around it . . .

·

It often happens that I ask myself whether the granting of a wish actually has anything to do with wishes themselves. As long as a wish is weak, it is like one-half of something that needs its being granted as its second half to amount to something independent and whole. But wishes can expand so wonderfully into something that is whole, complete, and intact and that without outside assistance grows into and assumes its shape entirely from within. A particular life's greatness and intensity might be attributed precisely to its willingness to entertain excessive wishes that would drive as if from the inside action after action, effect after effect into life without much recollection of these wishes' original aim and intent. Purely elemental, they transformed themselves like cascading water into decisive and genuine acts, immediate existence and cheerful optimism, all depending on what various occurrences and opportunities required.

·

I have often wondered whether especially those days when we are forced to remain idle are not precisely the days spent in the most profound activity. Whether our actions themselves, even if they do not take place until later, are nothing more than the last reverberations of a vast movement that occurs within us during idle days.

In any case, it is very important to be idle with confidence, with devotion, possibly even with joy. The days when even our hands do not stir are so exceptionally quiet that it is hardly possible to raise them without hearing a whole lot.

·

To come to agree with what is great and to allow it to be valid is nothing but an insight; to celebrate it, however, is exuberance because there what is great appears transfigured and cannot be surpassed. To apply it in one's interactions with others constitutes wisdom and spells the utmost success. But the task of all tasks is to transform what is insignificant into greatness, what is inconspicuous into radiance; to present a speck of dust in a way that shows it to be part of the whole so that one cannot see it without also instantly seeing all of the stars and the heavens' deep coherence to which it intimately belongs.

·

The widely asked question whether one "believes in god" (as we hear it today) seems to me based on the wrong premise, as if god could be reached at all by means of human striving and overcoming. The term *belief* has acquired the meaning of something strenuous; especially within Christianity it has assumed this connotation to a degree that one might fear that a kind of reluctance toward god is the soul's original state. But nothing could be less true. Anyone may take stock of the moment when his interaction with god originates in inexpressible rapture; or he might seize in profound reflection upon one often inconspicuous instant where he had first been moved by god, independent of the influences of his surroundings and often in opposition to them. It will be difficult to identify a life where this experience does not strongly impose itself sooner or later, but it imposes itself with such immeasurably gentle force that most people, being pressured by more explicit realities, do not register it. Or at least it does not enter their mind that this could be a fact of religion because they have been raised to receive religious stimuli only within shared conventions and not where their most solitary and proper essence is in question. And just as the development of a relation to god is blocked by the attitude of religious communities and churches, which preempt the individual's experience with their statutes and promises and actually distract him from those occasions that would prompt him to become productive in a religious sense, the individual is similarly swept away by the course of conventions in his attitude toward death and frequently lacks the strength to remain at the spot where he could develop his own death experiences in relation to the defining events of his life. The question regarding a "life after death" becomes meaningless as soon as we have to admit that what we summarize with the term *life* includes only the experiences of the here and now which remain attached to this "here" and to our senses of its perception to such a degree that we would have to find a completely different designation for any "other" life. Such a designation is already given with the term *death,* which without presumptiveness or curiosity we may assume to mean everything outside of our earthly existence. Throughout time there have always been those who thought that they had sufficient proof that this so-called death signifies an end, a condition of decay and the harsh disintegration of all living matter, but the very opposite opinion has also always found its supporters and defenders, and they have gone so far as to define death as a more intensive degree of life. Its immobility is then cited as proof of the greater intensity of vibration to which death, consequently more alive than we are, is subject. Our everyday perception would not contradict this: for instance, we still feel the movements of a high-speed train with our entire body while according to our experience we should have to interpret the vastly greater speed of the earth as a standstill.

To me (since you ask), it has seemed probable from my youth that death is nothing less than the opposite and refutation of life; my inclination always tended toward making it into the center of life as if we would be housed and sheltered in it quite well as if in the greatest and most profound intimacy. I cannot say that any experience has ever contradicted this assumption; yet I have also always refrained from imagining this being-in-death in any way, and all existing descriptions of a "beyond" have always left me quite indifferent. The tasks of our earthly existence are so numerous and the millennia of human existence, so far from mastering them, still seem so stuck in early discoveries that nothing seems to authorize us under these circumstances to guess the shape of any future condition instead of unreservedly applying ourselves to the present that is imposed on us for such a short time. I do not mean that we should ignore the secrets around us; but we should consider it our duty to understand how they relate to our current condition and not imprudently give up a point of view where all of our presently available advantages coincide. We do not even know yet how far we can reach from here but surely we increase our tension to the same degree to which we stabilize our position here.

•

When I entered your business in Winterthur for the first time, I felt quite distinctly but could not yet express what now moves me anew in reading this book [the history of a Swiss trading company]: the idea of trade in its humane immediacy and purity. This language used by continents among themselves whose carriers are the things that we use and value; these materials and what can be extracted and derived from them with care. And how this idea throughout its infinite application and inevitable complication over the centuries has forfeited none of its originality and youthfulness: how the lure of what is strange and remote remains one of its driving forces; the heartfelt curiosity in the joy of trading and the inexhaustible astonishment to encounter a product brought here from far away that is so different, so essentially valuable, so pure in its setting, so at one with its scent. And also *this* joy: to trade it in for something native that appears, according to its climate, more basic and inconspicuous.

•

If someone were to burst into song at the spot intended for him, even if that meant while working a machine or using a plow (which would be a quite privileged position!), that is of course acceptable; and yet it would be wrong to invoke people's professions constantly in order to invalidate the position of someone who writes as an artist (I avoid the horrid term *author of fiction*). Nobody would dream of pushing a rope maker, carpenter, or shoemaker away from their craft and "into life" so that they would become better rope makers, carpenters, or shoemakers. Musicians, painters, and sculptors likewise should be permitted to work in ways in which they are meant to work. Only in the case of the writer, the craft appears so insignificant, so *accomplished* from the beginning (anyone can write) that some are of the opinion that a writer left alone with his task would immediately indulge in free play! But what an error! To know how to write, god knows, is no less "difficult craftsmanship"—all the more so since the material used by other artists has from the beginning been set apart from its daily use, while the poet's task is heightened by the peculiar obligation to distinguish *his* word thoroughly and essentially from the words used in plain exchange and communication. *No* word in a poem (I here mean each *and* or *the* or *a*) is *identical* with the same-sounding word in a conversation. Its conformity to a purer set of laws and the way a word in verse or artistic prose is placed into a greater context and constellation: all these transform each word deep in the core of its nature, and render it useless, unusable for mere exchange, untouchable and lasting.

Art is directed against nature: it is the most passionate inversion of the world, the return path from infinity where all honest things now face us. There, on this path, they can now be seen in their entirety, their faces come closer and their movements become more distinct—but who are we to be *allowed* to proceed in this direction facing them all, to carry out this eternal reversal that deceives them by making them believe that we had already arrived somewhere, at some destination, and that now we can leisurely retrace our steps?

•

Places, landscapes, animals, things: in reality all of this knows nothing of us—we pass through it the way an image passes through a mirror. We pass through: this sums up our entire relation, and the world is shut off like an image; there is no place where we can enter. And yet this is why all of this is of such great help for us: the landscape, this tree leafed through by the wind, this thing surrounded by the afternoon and occupied with itself, like all things—because we cannot pull any of this with us into our uncertainty, into our danger, into our obscure and unenlightened heart, this is the reason why all of this helps us. Have you never noticed that this is the magic of art and its tremendous and heroic strength: that it mistakes us for this most alien dimension and transforms it into us and us into it, and that it shifts our suffering into things and reflects the unconscious and innocence of all things back into us out of rapidly turned mirrors?

•

Fame is nothing but the sum of all the misunderstandings that cluster around a new name . . . Wherever a human achievement becomes truly great, it seeks to hide its face in the lap of general, nameless greatness.

•

Fame today, in an age when everything is operated mechanically, is far from producing periods of quiet. Instead, once set in motion it creates the ruckus of an immense printing plant where it is impossible to hear one's own words over thousands of fame-wheels and fame-belts, and everyone who approaches the individual who is caught in them finds himself ultimately also pressed into service and soon contributes to the machine's monstrous actions and berserk roaring. Fame has to occur quickly in an era when its results are worn thin so rapidly; even the youngest people live among these fame-motors set up around them by a publisher and a few friends. It is quite rare to encounter a truly creative and productive person who resides in his own stillness or simply in the midst of his melody, close to the honest beating of his heart!

.

You know that what appears inexorable must be present [in poetry] for the sake of our greatest desires. Beauty will become paltry and insignificant when one looks for it only in what is pleasing; there it might be found occasionally but it resides and lies awake in each thing where it encloses itself, and it emerges only for the individual who believes that it is present everywhere and who will not move on until he has stubbornly coaxed it forth.

.

No one can lift so much beauty out of himself that it would conceal him entirely. A part of his being always remains visible behind it. But in times of greatest artistic achievement individuals have accumulated such a great and noble inheritance in addition to their beauty that the work no longer has any need for them. Curiosity and the habits of the audience search for and detect a personality; but there is no need for that. In such times, there exists art but no artists.

ON DIFFICULTY AND ADVERSITY

The Measure by Which
We May Know Our Strength

A failure ought not to be a disappointment for those who take on the most extreme challenges and do not settle comfortably in what is modestly proportioned; it is the calibrated measure of our endeavors that is not even meant to be referred to our feelings or to be used as evidence against our achievement, which after all incessantly reconstitutes itself from a thousand new beginnings.

Apparently the power to establish order, which ranks among the most inexorable strengths of artistic creation, is summoned most insistently by two interior states: by one's awareness of abundance and by the utter collapse within a human being, which, after all, yields yet another abundance.

To feel completely apathetic, when it includes even one's emotions, is nature's way of retreating and escaping; it is a violent measure taken by nature in order to be left alone.

The experience of something that has been thwarted is surely matched on the other side by something that has been unexpectedly fulfilled.

But of course one never knows with an individual whether he might not suddenly, even in spite of himself, discover the point from which he can gather himself into a new and coherent unity.

This "task" is actually always there: it's only that we, distracted by names, sometimes don't recognize it in its namelessness.

•

I realize with a sense of dread that one grows numb with regard to even the most wonderful things when they become part of one's daily interactions and surroundings.

•

This is not to say that one ought to weaken the impact of what is difficult or to take it less to heart so that it can be properly assimilated. On the contrary, the more fully we experience what is difficult, the more it pulls and drives us with its weight toward the center of life. And life's gravitational field is oriented so centripetally that only if someone makes himself light by artificial means could he become estranged from it. No matter how horrified we may be by our detachment from what is reliable or familiar or beloved—which is called error, joy, or separation—we ultimately experience (if we only practice the most patient forbearance) such a complete, unshakable, even sublime *being-part-of-the-whole* that each instance when we miss it or depart from it seems only like a slight sensory illusion. And many of those instances taken together constitute the kind of preliminary reality that we are able to replace only gradually with the actual realities of our larger relations.

•

All of misery is always present and all of suffering, including the most extreme. There is surely, we tell ourselves, all of misery and all of suffering in full use at any given moment among humans, as much as there is all taken together. It is a fixed constant just as there is a fixed constant of happiness; only the distributions vary.

•

In life one cannot awaken often enough the sense of a beginning within oneself. There is so little external change needed for that since we actually transform the world from within our hearts. If the heart longs for nothing but to be new and unlimited, the world is instantly the same as on the day of its creation and infinite.

●

This "taking life the hard way" with which my books are filled—this is not at all melancholy (and this "terrible" and that "consoling" that you have so affectionately embraced will move ever closer together in these books until it finally becomes *One* in them, their only essential content)—this not-taking-things-lightly is intended to be nothing else, right?, but a taking stock according to the true weight: that is, a true taking in of reality, an effort to weigh things in carats of the heart and not according to suspicion, luck, or chance. No refusal, right?!, *no refusal;* ah, on the contrary, how much endless affirmation and always more affirmation of existence!

●

Somewhere in space there must be sites where even that which is monstrous appears to be something natural, one of the rhythmic upheavals of the universe that is secured in its existence even at the point where we are doomed.

●

One must never despair upon losing something, whether it is an individual or an experience of joy or happiness; everything returns even more magnificently. What *has to* decline, declines; what belongs to us, stays with us, for everything works according to laws that are greater than our capacity for understanding and that only seem to contradict us. You have to live within yourself and think of *all* of life, all of its millions of possibilities, openings, and futures in relation to which there exists nothing that is past or has been lost.

•

The most divine consolation is without a doubt contained within the human itself. We would not know very well what to do with the consolations of a god. All that is necessary is for our eye to be a trace more seeing, for our ear to be more receptive, for the flavor of a fruit to enter us more completely, for us to be able to tolerate more scent, and, in touching and being touched, to be more present-minded and less oblivious—in order to receive from our most immediate experiences consolations that would be more convincing, more significant and truer than any suffering that can ever unsettle us.

•

It is dispiriting to think *what* kind of things people turn to in their helpless, disoriented curiosity about themselves. Especially since everything about us originates in this state of not-knowing-ourselves.

•

Are there circumstances of the heart that include the greatest horrors for the sake of being complete, because the world is not world until *Everything* occurs within it?

•

How every creature is basically confronted with only *that* heaviness that exists on a level with its proper strengths, even if it then often vastly exceeds them.

We, however, being placed at the incomprehensible intersection of so many different and mutually contradictory surroundings, we are suddenly assaulted by a difficulty that has no connection whatsoever with our knowledge or its uses: by an *alien* difficulty.

(When would a swan be forced to undergo one of the lion's ordeals? How could a piece of fish-fate enter the bat's being, or the fright of a horse a digesting snake?)

•

The suffering that has defined the existence of mankind from the beginning of time cannot actually be intensified by any means. But it is certainly possible to intensify our insight into mankind's unspeakable suffering, and this might yet lead to: so much decline— as if new beginnings were in the process of creating the distance and space they need to occur.

•

The most wonderful aspect of life still seems to me that some coarse and crude intervention and even a blatant violation can become the occasion for establishing a new order within us. This is indeed the most superb achievement of our vitality: that it interprets evil as something good and quite actually inverts the two. Without this kind of magic we would all be evil since evil touches and invades everyone. Anyone could be caught in a specific moment of being "bad"; only that one not stay put, *that* is the secret, that one continues to *live*. Nothing is more unsustainable than what is bad. This is why no one ought to think that he might "be" bad; he need only shift ever so slightly and he is no longer "bad."

•

What a horrible state *those* are in who long to have an experience. Why do they do it? Because they could not cope with some early and then the third and fourth experience, and failed to assimilate it by truly dissolving it—that is why they continue to chase after the kind of experience for which they are no match. And it is by the grace of god alone if they remain only always in pursuit and if each new catch eludes them.

•

And yet, is this not what life is? This is what I think: that the countless paltry, timid, petty, and shameful details ultimately still amount to a wonderful whole—a whole that would not exist if it depended upon us to understand and achieve it, but to which we contribute in equal parts with our abilities and failures.

•

"Who would renounce jubilation?" I once wrote in a forgotten poem. Indeed: rejoicing cannot be renounced. Once a heart has been turned on to experiencing life's innermost intensity—not only life in the so-called here and now but probably all being in its entirety—such a heart must consider itself completely fulfilled and privileged, even if the one who would be entitled to receive proof of this intensity turns away. (He himself loses something infinite by being kept for some reason from eliciting such proof over and over again.) To say it in the language of today: maybe such a heart can be called "unhappy," and yet it will spontaneously have effects on everything of which it is a part. These effects will correspond to its actual and higher condition from which it cannot lapse again.

•

And while I considered all of the disturbances that the calamitous [war] years had caused others and myself, I also arrived at what seems like a valid response to the question regarding the famous "difficulties" that people are so often inclined to present as educational and productive. I think there ought to be *one* great, tremendous prayer that wishes for everyone to encounter on his path only that which is difficult for *him,* by which I mean *that* which is at least somehow proportionate with those tasks in his life that he has understood and passionately affirmed: this may then be great, even extraordinarily overpowering; it could even be fatal. For is there anyone, once he has accepted to fight a genuine struggle, who does not also feel a quiet sacred joy in perishing in it . . . but *in* it, not outside of it, not on terrain where his best, most serious, and most practiced skills, his strengths, his judgment, his accumulated experience seem paralyzed or never attain any relevance. Is *this* not the proper way of answering the question? Especially as far as the artist is concerned whose tasks absolutely and unreachably exceed him precisely on that terrain where he is most authentic. One would wish and indeed grant *him* above all others to be confronted (if possible, beginning in his youth) with nothing but *his* difficulties!

The strings of sorrow may only be used extensively if one vows to play on them also at a later point and in their particular key all of the joyousness that accumulates behind everything that is difficult, painful, and that we had to suffer, and without which the voices are not complete.

Whatever is heavy and difficult, as long as it is only borne properly, also marks the precise weight of life. It teaches us the measure by which we may know our strength and which we may then also apply when we feel blessed with happiness.

It is confusing to no end that so much difficulty and pain originate in the ultimately superfluous and unnecessary distortions and paralyses of existence, which for times immemorial have resulted from the nonwakefulness, sluggishness, and narrowness of human circumstances and which have been heaped in great quantities on that which is actually life's happiness. We live underneath the debris of institutions that fell into ruin long ago, and whenever we find a way out there may be the pure sky above but still no order around us, and then we stand even more isolated and threatened by the daily danger of sudden new collapses. Sometimes I cannot look at several people together, not even complete strangers toward whom I am entirely indifferent, without realizing with the deepest internal fright how very much they act in falsehood. When they begin to talk simply to escape the embarrassment caused by their mutual strangeness and silence (which is considered impolite), and when they really find words for hours, whole bundles of words that sound as if they had been bought cheaply at auction, how time passes then: And yet this evening is an irreplaceable hour of their lives. And yet they are surrounded everywhere by sublime nature, which ought to summon anyone who innocently raises his eyes to great thoughts and vast feelings. And yet each one of them faces a night that will scare him with its unmastered depths and urgently impose on him the disasters from which he averts his eyes, the failures for which he does not make up, his unacknowledged grief. A night during which he is even more than usually the property and plaything of his death, this death that he despises and denies before his own blood that courses in sweet and intimate agreement with it.

•

Among lonely people there is not a single one who can be sure that in his suffering he might not yet console someone else and that the gestures of his most personal helplessness, like so many cues and signals, might not serve as signs guiding the way in the realm of the unfathomable.

ON CHILDHOOD AND EDUCATION

This Joy in Daily Discovery

Childhood—what actually was it? What *was* it, this childhood? Is there any other way of asking about it except with this helpless question—what was it?: that burning, that being amazed, that incessant not-being-able-to-help-oneself, that sweet, that profound, that beaming feeling-of-tears-welling-up? What was it?

Most people do not know at all how beautiful the world is and how much magnificence is revealed in the tiniest things, in some flower, in a stone, in tree bark, or in a birch leaf. Adults, being preoccupied with business and worries and tormenting themselves with all kinds of petty details, gradually lose the very sight for these riches that children, when they are attentive and good, soon notice and love with all their heart. And yet the greatest beauty would be achieved if everyone remained in this regard always like attentive and good children, naïve and pious in feeling, and if people did not lose the capacity for taking pleasure as intensely in a birch leaf or a peacock's feather or the wing of a hooded crow as in a great mountain range or a magnificent palace. What is small is not small in itself, just as that which is great is not—great. A great and eternal beauty passes through the whole world, and it is distributed justly over that which is small and that which is large; for in important and essential matters, there exists no injustice anywhere on earth.

Art is childhood.

.

There is really no more beautiful way of putting one's own life force to the test than by recognizing and seizing joy itself, without exaggeration but purely with the strength of joy, and to grasp with its proper measure the perfection and loveliness of a few days without even the least sense of a "too much." A child, after all, does nothing but that, and we are always closest to the center of our lives at the point where according to our own means we most closely resemble the child!

.

Why, by god, does one spend one's life according to conventions that constrict us like a tight costume and that prevent us from reaching the invisible soul, this dancer among the stars!

.

We do not claim life by means of an "education" but only in those spots where there is devotion, reverence, a joyous resolve and an expansive heart. This is the question: does your heart yearn for *one* thing alone? And is this thing the theater in its greatest and most noble sense? And are you committed to this heart, which has thus risen for this *one* thing, for all of life and to the death? Or do you give yourself also to other things, and desires, and intentions? Here, now, examine yourself.

.

I maintain that we have made things much easier for our children and even spared them many things, frequently without any active attempt on our part, because certain facts that have become known through psychological discoveries, whether we are aware of them or not, have assumed an immediate reality within us. And we are much more likely to base our actions on this reality than on the principles and moralities that may still cling to us and that we think we have to maintain because of our "professional" obligation as parents, so to speak . . .

●

To have a childhood means to live a thousand lives before the one.

●

Childhood is a land entirely independent of everything. The only land where kings exist. Why go into exile? Why not grow older and more mature in this land? . . . Why get used to what *others* believe? Is there any more truth in that than in what one had believed with one's initial, strong child-faith? I can still remember . . . each thing having a particular meaning, and there were countless things. And none was worth more than any other. Justice reigned over them. There was a period when each thing seemed to be the only one, when every single one could become one's fate: a bird that flew in the night and now was sitting, dark and serious, in my favorite tree; a summer rain that transformed the garden so that all of its greenery seemed glazed with darkness and gleam; a book where a flower had been placed among the leaves, god knows by whom; a pebble of strange, interpretable shape: all of this was as if one knew much more of it than the grown-ups. It seems as if with each thing one could become happy and big but also as if one could perish on each thing . . .

●

This is finally true: deep on the inside everyone is like a church, and the walls are adorned with festive frescoes. In earliest childhood, when this magnificence is still exposed, it is too dark inside to see the images, and then, while the hall is gradually reached by light, adolescent foolishness and its false longings and thirsting shame set in and cover up wall after wall. Some people advance quite far into and through life without suspecting the original magnificence underneath the sober poverty. But blessed is he who senses, finds, and secretly recovers it. He presents himself with a gift. And he will return home to himself.

Parents should never want to teach us life; for they teach us *their* life.

In light of the current state of affairs, one can certainly say that good parents as much as bad parents, and good schools as much as bad schools, are in the wrong with regard to the child. They all fundamentally misrecognize the child by starting from the false premise of the adult who feels superior toward the child. They ought to recognize instead that the greatest individuals have always sought at specific moments to become an equal to and someone worthy of the child.

Ah, if our parents were only born with us, how much backtracking and bitterness we would be spared. But parents and children can only walk side by side, never together; there is a deep ditch between them across which they can pass to each other from time to time a little love.

Each person ought to be guided *only* to the point where he becomes capable of thinking by himself, working by himself, learning by himself. There are only very few great truths that one may voice in front of a group of individuals without insulting one among them: these are the only matters for school. Schools ought to think above all in terms of individuals and not in terms of grades: since life and death and fate are ultimately all intended for individuals. School needs to chart a relation to all of that, to the great and true experiences and events, if it hopes to regain its vitality.

How many children exist who later could experience life as abundant and whole, although for one reason or another they had been given nothing *more* on their way than "pure life." It is not the worst thing to be given only that and then to be placed among humans: strong, productive, even great things have risen from such defenselessness, which, if one is looking for a bit of consolation, is a much more immediate part of life than the self-opinionated state of protection in which most "sheltered" children grow up finally to be poor and limited!

Every historical period is filled with a burning desire for the great individuals who are different: for they have always brought with them the future. Yet when individuality surfaces in a child it is treated disdainfully or disparagingly or possibly—which is most painful for the child—with derision. They are treated as if they had nothing that was unique to them, and the deep riches out of which they live are devalued to offer them commonplaces instead. Even if one has stopped treating adults in this way, one remains intolerant and impatient with regard to children. The right that is naturally granted to any grown-up is denied to children: to have their own opinion. All of contemporary education amounts to an unending battle with the child in which both parties finally resort to the most reprehensible means. And schools continue only what the parents had already begun. It is a systematic battle against the child's personality. It despises the individual, his wishes and desires, and it considers its task to push this individual down to the level of the masses. One need only read the life-stories of all great individuals; they became great always *in spite of* school and not because of it.

·

As peculiar as this may sound under current conditions, in school life has to undergo a transformation. If life is anywhere to become broader, deeper, more human, this has to happen in school. Afterward, it quickly hardens in professions and fates, no longer has time to change, and has to work its effects the way it is. In school, however, there is time and quietness and space: time for every kind of development, quiet for every voice, space for all of life and all of its values and things.

A series of unspeakable errors has turned school into the opposite: increasingly, life and reality have been pushed out of it. School was supposed to be nothing but school, and life was something completely different. It was supposed to come only later, after school, and it was supposed to be something for adults (as if children were not alive, as if they were not in the center of life).

Due to this incomprehensible, unnatural strangulation, school has died off. All of its content has ossified into rigid clumps because it lacked the movements of life.

·

All knowledge that school has to offer ought to be distributed enthusiastically and generously, without restriction and reservations, unintentionally and by an impassioned individual. All subjects ought to deal with life as the one subject matter that is intended by all the other ones. Then all subjects would at their outer limits touch once again upon the great contexts which continually give birth to religion.

.

Don't children endure the most violent upsets so incredibly because they live in a state without expectation or suspicion and do not know that transformations *can* suddenly erupt?

.

I would like to believe that very small children experience themselves through tremendous intensities of pleasure, pain, and sleep. Later, then, there are periods when being in physical pain remains just about the only example of our own intensity, given how distractedly life deals with us.

.

Children *are at rest* in love (was I ever allowed to?), but then they are also pure in the state of deception that it would be possible to belong to someone. And whenever they say "mine," they do not make a claim of ownership but hold something tight and then let go, or when they actually hold on, then it is god—to whom they are still obscurely linked—who pulls everyone else toward him through these innocently open arms.

.

This is what it means to be young: this thorough faith in the most beautiful surprises, this joy in daily discovery.

.

Just think: is childhood not difficult in all of its unexplained contexts? Are the years of girlhood not difficult—don't they pull the head like so much long and heavy hair into the depth of great sadness? And nothing is *supposed* to change; if life then suddenly becomes more bearable, more carefree, and more joyful for many, this is only the case because they have stopped taking it seriously and actually bearing it and feeling it and filling it with their most authentic selves. This is not progress as life intends it. This is a renunciation of all of its expanses and opportunities. What is asked of us is that we *love what is difficult* and learn to handle what is difficult and heavy. In difficulty there are the benign forces, the hands that work on us. In the midst of difficulty we are meant to experience our joy, our happiness, our dreams: there, against the depth of this background, they become visible and only there we may recognize their beauty. And only in the darkness of difficulty our precious smile attains its meaning: only there it shines with its deep and dreamy light, and in the brightness that it spreads momentarily we behold the wonders and treasures all around us.

•

With only slight exaggeration I would say that we *are* not; we continually constitute ourselves anew and differently at the intersection of all those influences that reach into the sphere of our being.

•

There is no possibility of catching up with anything we missed, given how the world is both outside and inside so very full of that which is always most immediate.

On Nature

It Knows Nothing of Us

It is difficult to live in this world because there exists little love be-tween nature and man and between man and god. Man does not need to love either nature or god—but he has to comport himself in relation to him the same way nature does.

·

We play with dark forces that cannot be captured with the names we give them, like children playing with fire, and it seems for a moment as if all energy had rested dormant in all objects until now, until we arrived to apply it to our fleeting life and its require-ments. But, again and again throughout millennia, those forces shake off their names and rise like an oppressed class against their little masters, or not even *against* them—they simply rise and the various cultures slide off the shoulders of the earth, which is once again great and expansive and alone with its oceans, trees, and stars.

What does it mean that we transform the outermost surface of the earth, that we groom its forests and meadows and extract coal and minerals from its crust, that we receive the fruits from the trees as if they were meant for us, if we were only to recall even a sin-gle hour when nature acted beyond us, beyond our hopes, beyond our lives, with that sublime highness and indifference that fill all of its gestures. It knows nothing of us. And whatever human beings might have accomplished, not one has yet reached such greatness that nature shared in his pain or would have joined in his rejoicing. Sometimes nature accompanied great and eternal hours of history with its mighty, roaring music, or the winds seemed to stop when a decision was pending, all nature standing still with bated breath, or it would surround an instant of harmless social happiness with waving blossoms, swaying butterflies and leaping winds—but only in order to turn away the next moment and to abandon the one with whom it had just seemed to share everything.

•

The final and most profound element of which the great objects of art have been made exists in all of nature; it grows with every field, every skylark knows of it, and nothing else but *it* forces the trees into full bloom. Yet in nature it is concealed (while in objects of art it is held up in a breathless silence—like a monstrance); it is scattered about and nearly lost (while art objects contain it: gathered, recovered, preserved forever). And the difficult, arduous path of our development, obstructed in hundreds of ways, entails the recognition of greatness, spiritual necessity, and infinity ultimately in those areas where it cannot be captured in a single glance, where it is nearly impossible to seize it altogether except if one toils like Cinderella. Life is severe and unyielding like the stepmothers and evil queens of the fairy tale, but it also harbors those sweet and diligent forces that ultimately will finish the tasks for those who are patient and good but who cannot master them alone.

•

What we experience as spring, god views as a fleeting, tiny smile that passes over the earth. The earth seems to be remembering something, and in the summertime she tells everyone about it until she grows wiser during that great autumnal silence with which she confides in those who are alone. Even when taken together, all the springs that you and I have experienced are not enough to fill even one of god's seconds. The spring that god is supposed to notice must not remain in the trees and meadows but somehow has to assume its force within people, for then it takes place, as it were, not in time but in eternity and in god's presence.

ON SOLITUDE

The Loneliest People Above All
Contribute Most to Commonality

As a child, when I was being treated poorly by everyone, when I felt so infinitely abandoned, so absolutely lost in the unknown, there might have been a time when I longed to be elsewhere. But then while other human beings continued to be alien to me, I was drawn to things, and from these things there emanated a joy, a joy in being that always stayed consistently calm and strong and in which there was never any hesitation or doubt. In military school, after anxious, drawn-out struggles, I gave up my passionate Catholic child-piety, freed myself from it in order to be all the more inconsolably alone. Things, however, in their way of patiently enduring and lasting, later offered me a new, greater, and more pious love, a kind of belief with neither fear nor limit. Life also belongs to this belief. Ah, how I believe in it, in life. Not the life constituted by time but this other life, the life of small things, the life of animals and of the great plains. This life that continues through millennia with no apparent investment in anything, and yet with all of its forces of movement and growth and warmth in complete harmony. This is why cities weigh on me so heavily. This is why I love taking long barefoot walks where I will not miss a grain of sand and will make available to my body the entire world in many shapes as sensation, as experience, as something to relate to. This is why I exist, wherever possible, on vegetables alone, in order to come close to a simple awareness of life unaided by anything alien. That is why I will not drink wine, because I want nothing but my juices to speak out and rush through me and attain bliss, the way they do in children and animals, from deep within the self! And this is also why I want to strip myself of all arrogance and not consider myself superior to the tiniest animal or any more wonderful than a stone. But to be what I am, to live what I was meant to live, to want to sound like no one else, to yield the blossoms dictated to my heart: this is what I want—and this surely *cannot* be arrogance.

•

Whether you are surrounded by the singing of a lamp or the sounds of a storm, by the breathing of the evening or the sighing of the sea, there is a vast melody woven of a thousand voices that never leaves you and only occasionally leaves room for your solo. To know *when you have to join in,* that is the secret of your solitude, just as it is the art of true human interaction: to let yourself take leave of the lofty words to join in with the one shared melody.

•

The loneliest people above all contribute most to commonality. I have said earlier that one person might hear more and another less of the vast melody of life; accordingly, the latter has a smaller or lesser duty in the great orchestra. The individual who could hear the entire melody would be at once the loneliest and the most common, for he would hear what no one else hears and yet only because he would grasp in its perfect *completeness* that which others strain to hear obscurely and only in parts.

•

I have little to add except the following, which is valid in all cases: the advice, perhaps, to take solitude seriously and whenever it occurs to experience it as something good. The fact that other people fail to alleviate it should not be attributed to their indifference and withholding but because we are truly infinitely alone, each one of us, and unreachable with very rare exceptions. We must learn to live with this fact.

I consider the following to be the highest task in the relation be-tween two people: for one to stand guard over the other's solitude. If the essential nature of both indifference and the crowd consists in the nonrecognition of solitude, then love and friendship exist in order to continually furnish new opportunities for solitude. And only those commonalities are true that rhythmically interrupt deep states of loneliness . . .

In such a case [of a fight] it is time (in my personal opinion) to withdraw into oneself and to approach neither the one nor the other person and to resist referring the suffering caused by them back to the cause of suffering (which lies so far outside), but to make it productive for yourself. If you move what happens inside your feelings into solitude and keep your wavering and trembling sensations out of dangerous proximity to magnetic forces, then it will assume on its own its most natural and necessary position. In any case, it helps to remind oneself very frequently that everything that exists is governed by laws that reign over all beings without ever relinquishing their force, but rather rush to prove and test themselves on every stone and every feather dropped by us. When-ever we are in error, then, such erring is nothing but the failure to recognize that we are governed by specific laws in every single case. Every attempt of a solution will begin with our attention and focus that quietly integrate us into the chain of events and restore to our will its swaying counterweights.

One may be much more literal in one's dealings with a solitary in-dividual. In a sense, the spaciousness to which he would otherwise not gain any relation is delimited from being something truly immeasurable by another person's insights. But for someone who experiences life as a series of happy exchanges with others, the realm of existence is filled with realities, and such a person should be neither kept back at one discovery nor already set in anticipation for the next. His activity actually runs counter to that of the solitary individual: it is centrifugal and its gravitational effects are incalculable.

•

Incidentally, if I were young today, I would absolutely look for a daily, very heterogeneous way of applying myself and try to install myself in a tangible domain to the best of my abilities. Art today might be served better and more discreetly when it becomes the quiet affair of certain special days or years (which does not have to mean that it has to be carried out on the side or amateurishly; [Stéphane] Mallarmé, to cite the highest example, had been a teacher of English all of his life), but the "profession" itself is overcrowded with intruders, with interlopers, with exploiters of the increasingly hybridized trade, and it can be renewed and reinvested with meaning only by the quiet solitary *individuals* who do *not* consider themselves part of it and who accept none of the customs brought into circulation by literary authors. Whether as a private individual or by remaining inconspicuous behind a well-executed trade, the writer will be all the more likely to correct conditions that have long become impossible if his poetic *silence* will then carry a certain significance next to his most profound eloquence.

•

Everyone should find the center of his life in his work and be able to grow outward from this point as far as possible. And while he is thus engaged he should not be observed by anyone else, and especially not by the individual who is closest and dearest to him: for even he himself must not do that. There is a kind of purity and virginality in this looking away from one's self: it is just as when one is drawing with one's eyes locked on and intertwined with an object in nature, and the hand traces its path somewhere down there all alone, moves and moves, grows timid, wavers, regains confidence, moves and moves deep beneath the face which is like a star above it, which does not look but only *shines*. It seems as if I had always been creative in this way: the face caught in the contemplation of distant things, the hands alone. And this is surely how it ought to be. This is the way I would gradually like to become again, but in order to do so I have to remain as alone as I am now; my loneliness first has to be firm and secure again like a forest where no one ever set foot and which has no fear of steps. It must lose all emphasis, exceptionality, and obligation. It must become routine, completely natural and quotidian. The thoughts that enter, even the most fleeting ones, must find me all alone; then they will decide to trust me again.

Solitude is truly an *interior* affair, and to realize this insight and to live accordingly amounts to the best and most helpful form of progress. This is ultimately a matter of things that are not quite in our control, and success, which is after all so simple, is comprised of thousands of factors: we never quite know of what.

It happens only rarely that an individual gains a deeper and more serious understanding of himself during a happy and fulfilling time in his life; at such moments, most people dismiss the outcomes of their preceding solitude as gloomy errors and throw themselves into the blinding glare of happiness where they forget and deny the contours of their inner reality.

•

It is more than enough for one's entire existence to have a few, five, six, maybe nine, genuine experiences that return continually and in always new guises to the center of our heart. I can remember how I suffered the most amazing embarrassment as a young person when I had secured an hour of solitude in my room by explaining, in response to the curiosity that is typical of family life, why I needed this hour and *what* I intended to do with it: this was enough to make the hard-won solitude worthless from the start as if it had been sold in advance. The tone that had settled on this hour thwarted its innocence, claimed it and made it infertile and empty, and even before I had set foot in my room my treason had already arrived there and filled it to each corner with depletion, obviousness, and desolation.

•

Poet or painter, musician or architect, all solitary individuals at bottom who turn to nature because they prefer the eternal to the transient, the profound rhythms of eternal laws to that which finds justification in passing. Since they cannot persuade nature to share in their experience they consider their task to grasp nature in order to place themselves somewhere in its vast contexts. And with these single solitary individuals all of humanity approaches nature. It is not the ultimate and yet possibly the most peculiar value of art that it constitutes the medium in which man and landscape, figure and world encounter and find each other. In truth they live alongside one another, largely oblivious of each other. But in the painting, the building, the symphony—in a word, in art itself, they seem to join together as if in a higher, prophetic truth, to rely on one another, and it is as if they completed each other to become that perfect unity that characterizes the essence of the work of art.

•

To be alone is a veritable elixir that drives an illness completely to the surface. First it has to get bad, worse, the very worst—there is no going further in any language—but then all gets well.

•

Art is not a making-oneself-understood but an urgent understanding-of-oneself. The closer you get in your most intimate and solitary contemplation or imagination (vision), the more has been achieved, even if no one else were to understand it.

•

How stubbornly everything conspires to interrupt the creative individual and to withdraw and prevent him from his going-into-himself; how everything condemns the artist when he urgently desires to tend to and perfect his most interior world so that it may one day balance out and, as it were, become the counterpart to everything outside of us, everything, up to the stars. And even the friends who observe such an interior existence with indulgence and support, how frequently they fall prey to the error that, because they are giving something, they might in return receive something spiritual from the creative person that is *outside* of his work.

•

The art object can neither change nor improve anything; as soon as it has come into existence it presents itself to the human being no differently than nature, entirely self-sufficient, preoccupied with itself (like a fountain), and thus, if you prefer to call it that: indifferently. And yet we know that this second, withholding nature, which is itself held back by the will that determines it, nevertheless has been created out of what is human, out of the extremes of suffering and joy. And this is where we find the key to that treasure-vault of inexhaustible consolation, which seems to have accumulated in the artwork and to which a lonely person above all has a specific and ineffable claim. There are, I know this well, moments in life and maybe even years when loneliness among one's peers reaches a degree that one would not have admitted if it had been pointed out to us during periods of unforced, effortless social contacts. Nature is not capable of reaching us, and we have to have the strength to reinterpret and attract it to us, to translate it, as it were, into human terms to relate its smallest part to us. Yet this is precisely what one cannot do when one has become profoundly lonely: in such a state one wants to receive unconditional gifts and cannot cooperate at all, just as a human being at a certain low point of his vitality hardly wants to open his mouth to receive a bite of food. Whatever it is that intends and ought to reach us must overwhelm us as if it longed for us, as if it had no other purpose but to overpower this existence in order to transform each of the atoms of its weakness into devotion. And even then, strictly speaking, nothing has been changed. It surely would be presumptuous to expect an artwork to be able to help. But that the human tensions that are contained within a work of art without being directed toward the outside, that this inner intensity that is never rendered exterior could create the illusion that inside the work there is striving, challenge, courtship—, urgent rapturous love, turmoil, calling: that is the artwork's good conscience (not its purpose). And this deception that takes place between the work of art and an abandoned individual is no different from all of those priestly deceptions by means of which the divine had been promoted from the beginning of time.

•

Why do people in love break up before it becomes necessary to do so? Indeed, perhaps because this necessity may arise and become imperative at any moment. Because it is so very transient to be together and to be in love. Because behind it there lurks in everyone the peculiar certainty—this is admitted as often as it is denied—that everything that exceeds a pleasant and unchanging medium state will ultimately have to be received, endured, and mastered by an infinitely solitary (and almost singular) individual without any assistance from anyone else. The hour of dying during which this insight is wrested from everyone is nothing but one of our hours, and not an exception. Our being continually passes through and into transformations that might be no lesser in intensity than the new, near, and next states ushered in by death. And just as we must take leave of one another irrevocably at a specific instant during this most conspicuous of changes, strictly speaking we must surrender, let be and let go of each other with each passing moment. Does it disturb you that I can write all this down as if copying a sentence in a foreign language without any apparent awareness of the great pain that is thus expressed? I can do so because this terrible truth is probably at the same time our most productive and blissful truth. Although it loses none of its severe sublimity even when we contemplate it frequently (and even if one were to curl up around it tearfully, one would neither warm nor mollify it), our faith in its strength and difficulty grows every day. And suddenly one can just make out, as if glimpsed through clear tears, the distant realization that even as a lover one needs to be alone. This realization might be painful but it is not unjust, even when this need to be alone seizes and encloses us just at the moment when our feelings are surging toward the beloved. It is the realization that even this apparently most intimately shared thing called love can be fully developed and, as it were, perfected only when one is alone, apart from others. For the confluence of strong inclinations results in a current of pleasure that sweeps us along and finally casts us out somewhere else, while an individual enclosed in his feelings will experience love as a daily task to be performed on himself and as the incessant creation of bold and magnanimous challenges imposed on the other. People who are thus in love with each other summon infinite dangers, but they remain safe from the petty perils that have worn out and eroded so many great beginnings of true emotion. Since they continually wish for and challenge each other to achieve something extreme, neither of them can treat the other unjustly by imposing a limit; on the contrary, they incessantly create for one another space and expansiveness and freedom, just as the one who loves god has always flung from his heart and instituted in the depths of the heavens god's boundlessness and reign. That illustrious beloved has had the cautious wisdom and even (it cannot be misunderstood when phrased this way) used the noble ruse of never revealing himself. Thus for a few ecstatic souls the love of god could lead to imaginary moments of pleasure—and yet, according to its essence, it has always remained work through and through, a most demanding chore and a most difficult effort.

ON ILLNESS AND RECOVERY

Pain Tolerates No Interpretation

Even a drawn-out and slow convalescence opens up so many new and unanticipated relations to existence that it may nevertheless become a pleasurable and generous period of life, in spite of all the deprivation it necessarily entails.

•

It is insufferable to be held back by one's body. I have never understood how people manage to benefit mentally or spiritually from any kind of illness. For me it is nothing but an insult whenever I get sick, and I cannot imagine except in the most extreme situation a great use of such suffering, when it has become immeasurable and turns into martyrdom. In such a state, then, there is virtually no other recourse but to cast into the soul that vastness of pain that can no longer be accommodated in the body. There pain instantly becomes sheer force, regardless of its origins, just as in the work of art difficulty and even ugliness manifest themselves as nothing but strength, resolve, and fullness of life in the pure existence they now assume. But to suffer bodily on a small scale, in specific places, is pointless, and something that prompts my concern, as a distraction would . . .

•

How dangerous and merciless is life up to the final moment, a well-tamed creature, and yet inside of it how many insatiable forces that threaten it like wild beasts.

•

I used to wonder sometimes why the saints were so determined to inflict physical suffering upon themselves. Now I understand that this desire for pain, up to and including the suffering of martyr-dom, originates in haste and the impatience to be no longer inter-rupted or disturbed even by the worst that could happen here on this side. There are days when I look at every living creature with the worry that it could suddenly erupt with a pain that would make it scream. So great is my fear of the many ways in which the body abuses the soul, which rests quietly in the animals and reaches safety only in angels.

.

I am not afraid of sickness since I do not wish to hold on to it but only to endure it, to survive it. Being sick seems to me nothing but nature's cheerless need to figure out a way through all of these fuzzy multiplications back toward wholeness and health: she tries to do that to the best of her abilities. I think as long as one does not misunderstand illness by coddling it, there is nothing more infirm than pathology. Sickness itself is filled with the desire to be unreal, to be gone as soon as something secure can take its place.

.

It is true that even happiness can sometimes serve as a pretext for initiating us into that which by its very nature surpasses us. But, in such cases, it is far easier to understand instantly that something good is happening to us, even if the difficulty of *making use* of this good that we receive through happiness is no smaller than that of divining what could be positive at the bottom of those absences imposed on us by pain. We must advance in this region with far greater determination, and above all we must commit ourselves to destroying this old inherited suspicion that separates us from the best part of our own strengths, which we eye with such suspicion that we allow them to become strange—for they offer or impose on us, depending upon the circumstances, other means to endure than those which we consider compatible with our personality. Blessed moment of inner life when one either decides or devotes oneself to loving from now on unwaveringly and with all one's strength *that* which one fears the most, that which—according to our own measure—has made us suffer *too much*.

There is nothing more joyous than being able to truly make use of oneself again, whether in the service of plans or of memories; and what is most beautiful is the moment when plans and memories coincide and produce the desire and freedom to continue the one in the other.

[There is] that which we all know, this peculiar insurmountable disconnection between bodily suffering and its mental opposite, the incomprehensibility of physical pain, which we cannot resist "interpreting" and to which we seem to surrender in our very essence even though it is nothing but a misunderstanding, a contradiction, a reluctance, a desperate effort of our joyous nature to retain control, this nature that is in absolute agreement with us and committed to our existence. [Michel Eyquem de] Montaigne's impressions at the bedside of his painfully and wretchedly dying friend is the only other document known to me that has presented this conflict as profoundly as these honest, truthful sheets written by a mother [Gertrud Ouckama Knoop's description of her dying daughter, Vera, to whom Rilke dedicated *Sonnets to Orpheus*] who had the patience and strength (formed in Russia) not to look away but to experience even the cruelest moments with truly open eyes because these moments had now become her child's horrendous

property, her ultimate, fatal endowment brimming with infinite se-
crets . . . This I saw already in Montaigne a long time ago. Once a
close or beloved person is concerned, most people would suppress
such suffering along with all of its details and take recourse instead
to their vague emotions. When someone *possesses* the quiet deter-
mination to remain *objectively* receptive even in the face of such af-
fliction, then something like a first tentative inkling arises next to
all hopelessness and practically in the center of horror itself. This
presupposition occurs long before its time as if it were something
of a privilege that the human being is not spared such tremendous
suffering, and as if its ruthlessness signified something like an ini-
tiation into or belonging to the furthest possibilities—as if this des-
perate suffering could afflict only a creature for which there shall be
no more secrets.

.

Illness is the means by which an organism sheds what is foreign to
it; all that needs to be done is to assist it in being sick, to have the
complete illness, and then to escape from it, for that constitutes its
progress.

.

Not to award *more* meaning to what happens than what it assumes
on its own; not to consider suffering from the outside, not to mea-
sure it and call it great, "great suffering" . . . For you cannot be sure
whether your heart did not also grow with it and whether this im-
mense fatigue is not actually the heart growing and expanding. To
have patience, patience, and not to judge when suffering, never to
judge as long as one is bound up in suffering. One does not have a
measure for it; one makes comparisons and exaggerates.

.

For me, who have always been able to interact so agreeably with my nature and who have been used to reaching such positive agreements with it, the persistent need for a medical middleman is somehow confusing. For I feel how everything (including the most delicate preconditions of my artistic activity) depends on not letting the tracks of my own existence become blurred even when they pursue the wrong physical path. After all, the drive to art is nothing more than the persistent urge to achieve balance between the conflicts that jeopardize and strain our "Ego," which is continually reconstituted out of different and often contradictory elements. If it were only an illness that could be named with a precise Latin term, it would be fine for the medical expert to manage it; to permit him to intervene in the manifold, half-physical, half-psychic disaster where my suffering originates, however, is difficult and presents a risk. For everything I suffer is a task for myself, and so purely and exactly meant for my own work and ways of solving things that I am almost ashamed and have a bad conscience about involving the physician . . . I cannot even speak of taking him into confidence—for what could be confided in such a situation: half of it could be confided only to the friend of long ago (the one you refer to as my "comrade") and half of it would slip into wordless ness already within oneself. All coming-to-terms-with-oneself is so infinitely more productive than being helped, no matter by whom. Already as a child in the peculiar conditions into which I had been displaced, I had to experience that, and how often was it later confirmed for me when I witnessed individuals (sons against fathers, for instance, or married couples) who were numbingly and hopelessly locked in a fight in which they made each other increasingly sharp-edged, smaller and more deformed. I then realized that such a fight of the same intensity, when thrown *inside* an individual (who would then struggle with himself rather than another), would surely result in some kind of progress for this imagined solitary person!

·

No matter how much we would like to do so, it is quite difficult to assist one's doctor in reaching those deep regions where one advances oneself only by groping about. Perhaps one might also not permit oneself to grant a professional scientist access to these depths, even one with the best of intentions; one would surely prefer it if only life could provide the key to our most intimate depths, and then only to our friends. What is more, I have been my own doctor for too long not to develop some stupid jealousy toward the one who by his profession tries hard to know the secrets of my nature better than myself. Where does the body end that wants to yield so trustingly? Where does the soul begin that subsists on its own mystery? Will this ever be known?

·

In dying, it must often be the case that physical pain occurs as nothing but a malicious irritation. This must be the case because pain is surely most intimately linked to our here and now, and it is thus, as it were, invalid with regard to that general sphere toward which a dying person is beginning to orient himself. Pain's stubborn emphasis of a specific spot forces the dying individual into a one-sidedness that probably contradicts his inclination to attempt a kind of participation on an already worldly level, which of course must still be accomplished entirely with the means found here. But to acquire for ourselves the earthly means, to reach a certain completeness in our relations to the earth, to be here, ineffably, indescribably, breathlessly: would that not be the only way for us finally to be gathered into something greater than mere earthliness?

To take seriously and endow with great significance a small and actually insignificant object [such as a small stone], to invest it with (superstitious) belief—this is an indescribable experience for me, and when I have succumbed to such leanings I have never thought that they constitute an abuse of one's nature, even though I knew how easily such a stance could settle into a pathological state if we failed to keep our minds nimble. Upon reflection I have to agree with you; of course one behaves more freely when one can move beyond all similar temptations to reach pure independence. Which is probably precisely what one does when relying on such help, all of which retains a trace of transience and impermanence (besides its resemblance to god). I have always considered such small things illuminated by our heart's glow as the boundary stones of an otherwise unexplored realm which gradually comes within our reach and then is spontaneously picked up at the moment when we accidentally pass it. Should we really be judged so harshly when we continue to value this kind of mythologizing, now reduced to the level of a bourgeois interior? Since nearly all conditions of our inner, invisible experience exceed us by their very nature, it seems quite innocent to me if we occasionally take a willing object into our confidence and regard it as the carrier of powers that are yet to unfold within us. How many of the greatest achievements finally did not have such a small precaution as their precondition? Do you not think that superstitious belief (as long as it truly helps us and not vice versa, as if a pathology were being served by us) is nothing but a piece of prebelief, a runway leading into true belief—alas, all of this needs only to be alive; then there is no danger. After all, we will never get beyond pretexts, and when we presently charge something insignificant with being something more, it will return this authority to us precisely because of its insignificance. And upon its return will this power not finally appear slightly augmented, simply due to the object's simple virtue? Piggy banks: yes, from the start I had been thinking of them; that is what all of those talismans always seemed to me. They gather small batteries of life force, charged by us with what we otherwise give off into the randomly dispersing air.

.

Finally, it's nothing but nature's reluctance that causes all of our pain, and its resolve to establish balance, which it finds by way of suffering. Nature is completely unaware that it causes *us* pain while striving to establish order within itself and defend itself. And because nature does not take our consciousness into consideration, it becomes our task not to dissolve pain into consciousness; pain tolerates no interpretation. It appears that one has to let pain burn itself out wherever it happens, as it were, without trying to understand any matters of the mind or life in the light of its flickering blaze. Pain makes sense only on the side that it has turned toward nature; on the other side it is absurd, raw and unhewn material without any form or surface, ungraspable . . .

.

To endure and to have patience (this is how one gains experiences), to expect no help but truly great, almost miraculous help: this is what allowed me to go on since childhood. So also this time, although the suffering lasts a bit longer than usual, I do not wish to advance my nature by prodding it from the outside but simply want to wait, among one of the last ones, for it to make the decisive leap. This is the only way for me to know that this was my own genuine rather than borrowed strength, or even just an alien ferment that rises briefly only to fold murkily back in on itself . . .

Even—it seems to me—that which is called pathological, once lived through properly—that is, emphatically and for the sake of health—seems to me only a kind of clumsiness: and that which is great and has nothing to fear might be attracted and summoned even by this.

On Loss, Dying, and Death

Even Time Does Not "Console" . . .
It Puts Things in Their Place
and Creates Order

It has seemed to me for a long time that the influence of a loved one's death on those he has left behind ought to be none other than that of a higher responsibility. Does the one who is passing away not leave a hundredfold of everything he had begun to be continued by those who survive him—if they had shared any kind of inner bond at all? Over the past few years I have been forced to gain intimate knowledge of so many close experiences of death. But with each individual who was taken from me, the tasks around me have only increased. The heaviness of this unexplained and possibly mightiest occurrence, which has assumed the reputation of being arbitrary and cruel only due to a misunderstanding, presses us more deeply into life and demands the most extreme duties of our gradually increasing strengths.

•

We simply *do not know* what can be destroyed in a heart through suffering, or what suffering might achieve there. Suffering is certainly not constructive; at best, it puts up the scaffolding covered by tarps behind which the actual stones might assume the proper order. But then one must also admit that suffering will be quietly taken down once it is no longer absolutely needed, and one will refrain from attributing significance to the planks and boards and the posters and flyers that have gradually taken over this space. Only those are in the right who keep an open door for both good and ill, so that each may come but also leave according to its needs. To allow misery to get used to one, to slip it every day the sugar meant for one's coffee so that it finally lies under every table and no longer

wants to leave, means to train this phantom in ways that run coun-
ter to its rutting nature. As a poet, one should not even take distress
for a lover but move all of affliction and bliss into one's work, and
one's external life must be shaped by the refusal to suffer either af-
fliction or bliss anywhere else.

•

I once stood on a bridge in Paris and saw from a distance on a road
leading down to the river a suicide victim wrapped in oilcloth. He
had just been pulled dead from the Seine. Suddenly I heard some-
one next to me say something. It was a young blond carter in a blue
jacket, very young, strawberry blond, with a smart, clever, pointed
face. On his chin was a wart from which sprouted almost exuber-
antly a stiff bunch of red hairs like a paintbrush. Since I turned
toward him, he pointed with a nod of his head toward the object
that elicited our attention and said, winking at me: "Don't you
think, this one over there, since he was able to manage that, he
surely could have done still other things as well."

I followed him with my gaze, astonished, while he was already
walking back to his enormous cart filled with rocks, for truly: *what*
would one not be able to achieve with exactly that strength that is
necessary to untie the strong and mighty bonds of life! Since that
day, I know with absolute certainty that even the worst turn of
events, that even despair is only abundance, that it is an onslaught
of our being that could be forced in the opposite direction with
one single decision of the heart. Where something becomes ex-
tremely difficult and unbearable, there we also stand always already
quite near its transformation.

•

Words . . . could they be words of consolation? I am not sure about
that, and I don't quite believe that one could console oneself over

a loss as sudden and great as the one you just experienced. Even time does not "console," as people say superficially; at best it puts things in their place and creates order—and even that only because we so quickly begin to regard this order casually and consider it so little, this order to which time contributes so quietly by finding the proper place for, appeasing, and reconciling everything within the great Whole. Instead of admiring what has been placed there, we regard it as a result of our forgetfulness and the weakness of our heart simply because it no longer pains us acutely. Ah, how little it *forgets,* this heart—and how strong it would be if we did not deprive it of its tasks before they had been fully and genuinely achieved! Our instinct should not be to desire consolation over a loss but rather to develop a deep and painful curiosity to explore this loss completely, to experience the peculiarity, the singularity, and the effects of *this* loss in our life. Indeed, we should muster the kind of noble greed that would enrich our inner world with *this* loss and its significance and weight . . . The more profoundly we are affected by such a loss and the more painfully it concerns us, the more it becomes our *task* to claim as a new, different, and definitive possession that which has been so hopelessly emphasized by this loss. *This* amounts to the infinite achievement that instantly overcomes all the negative aspects of pain, all the sluggishness and indulgence that is always a part of pain. This is active, inner-working pain, the only kind that makes sense and is worthy of us. I don't love the Christian conceptions of a beyond, and I increasingly move away from them without, of course, thinking of attacking them; they may have their right to exist like so many other hypotheses of the divine periphery. For me, however, they present above all the danger of rendering our lost ones less concrete and initially less reachable, and when we move ourselves longingly toward this beyond and *away* from here, we are also rendered less precise, less earthly: a condition that for now and as long as we are *here* and related to tree, flower, and soil, we have yet to embrace purely and even yet still to attain! As far as I am concerned, what died for me died, so to speak, into my own heart: the vanished individual had gathered so strangely and surprisingly *inside* of me when I looked for him, and I was very moved to feel that he now existed nowhere any longer *except* there. My enthusiasm for serving, deepening, and glorifying his existence there gained the upper hand almost at the same moment when the pain would otherwise have attacked and devastated the entire landscape of my soul. If I recall how I loved my father—how I loved him often under extreme difficulties to understand and accept each other! During my childhood my thoughts were frequently confused and my heart froze at the mere thought that at some point he could cease to exist; my existence seemed to me so entirely determined by him (my existence which from the start had such a different purpose!) that his departure had for my inner nature the same significance as my own demise . . . but death is rooted *so* deeply in the essence of love (if we only shared *in* this knowledge of death, without being deterred by the ugliness and suspicions that have been attached to it) that it nowhere contradicts love. *Where,* finally, can death drive the one thing that we had carried in our heart with such wordless intensity if not *into* that very heart, where would be the "idea" of this beloved being and its unceasing influence (for *how* could *that* influence have ceased since already during that person's lifetime it had begun to work independently of his or her tangible presence) . . . *where* would this always secret effect be more secure than *within* us?! Where can we get closer to it, where can we celebrate it more purely, where can we submit to it better than there where it occurs in unison with our own voices as if our heart had mastered a new language, a new song, a new strength! I reproach all modern reli-

gions for supplying their believers with consolations and embel-
lishments of death instead of providing them with the means in
their soul to accommodate and reach an agreement with it. With
death, with its complete and unmasked cruelty: this cruelty is so
tremendous that it completes the circle: *it* reaches all the way to the
extremity of a gentleness that is great, pure, and utterly *transparent*
(all consolation is murky!), to a degree of gentleness that we would
not have imagined possible, even on the mildest spring day! But in
order to experience this most profound gentleness, which could
perhaps penetrate and make transparent all conditions of life even
if only a few of us would embrace it with conviction: in order to
prepare for the experience of *this* purest and most complete gentle-
ness, mankind has never embarked on even the first steps, except in
the most ancient and innocent times whose secrets have nearly
been lost. I am sure that the content of "initiations" had never
been anything but the communication of a "key" that allowed us
to read the word "death" *without* negation; just like the moon, life
surely has a side that is perpetually turned away from us and which
is not its opposite but adds to its perfection and completeness, to
the truly intact and full sphere of *being*.

We ought not to fear that our strength does not suffice for en-
during an experience of death, not even the closest and most hor-
rible one. Death is not *beyond* our strength; it is the highest mark
etched at the vessel's rim: we are *full* every time we reach it—and
being-full means (for us) being-weighed-down . . . that is all. I do
not mean to say that one should *love* death. But one should love life
so unreservedly and without any calculation or deliberation that
death (the half of life that is turned away from it) is at all times un-
wittingly included in and loved along with life—which is precisely
what happens each time in love's vast, unstoppable, and boundless
movements! Death has increasingly become something strange

only because we excluded it in a sudden fit of reflection, and, because we confined it to strangeness, it has become hostile.

It is possible that death is infinitely closer to us than life itself . . . What do we know of it?! Our effort (this had become increasingly clear to me over the years, and my work has maybe only this *one* purpose and task: to bear witness to this realization, which so frequently overwhelms me unexpectedly and always more impartially and independently . . . maybe more like a vision, if that does not sound too conceited) . . . our effort, I believe, can aim *only* at presupposing the *unity* of life and death so that it may gradually prove itself to us. Since we are prejudiced *against* death, we do not succeed in prying it out of its disfigurations . . . Believe me that death is a *friend,* our most profound friend, maybe the only one who is never, never deterred by our actions and indecision . . . and *this,* you understand, *not* in the sentimental-romantic sense of a denial of life, of the opposite of life, but our friend especially *then* when we most passionately, most tremblingly affirm our being-here, all that happens, nature, love . . . Life says always at the same time: Yes and No. Death (I implore you to believe it!) is the actual yes-sayer. He says *only:* Yes. Before eternity.

•

What, finally, would be more useless to me than a consoled life?

•

One never knows to what extent small and even the pettiest things might console and affirm us with regard to that which truly matters.

•

There is only *one* form of liberation for those who are continually submerged in suffering: to elevate suffering to the level of one's own perspective and to transform it into an aid for one's way of seeing.

•

My dear S . . . , I very much took your letter to heart, and, on the one hand, I wish to encourage you in your pain so that you experience it in all of its fullness, since as the experience of a new intensity it is a great experience of *life* and in turn leads back toward life, like everything that reaches a certain extreme degree of strength. On the other hand, I am filled with fear when I imagine how you have cut off and limited your life at this point, afraid of touching anything full of memories (and what is not full of memories?). You will freeze up if you keep doing that, you must not, dear, you have to keep moving, you have to return to the things that had been his, you have to lay hand on [your lost one's] things that are also yours due to such complex relations and attractions, S . . . (this might be the mission assigned to you by this incomprehensible fate). You *have to* continue his life *within* your life to the extent that it had not been completed; his life has now passed over to yours and you who truly knew him can move forward quite as he intended: make this the task of your mourning, to explore what he expected of you, hoped for you, wished would happen to you. If I could only convince you, my friend, that his influence has not left your existence (how much more securely I feel my father's influence and assistance within me since he is no longer with us). Consider how much in daily life distracts, obscures, and renders another's love imprecise. Now especially he is here, and now he has all the freedom to be here and we have all the freedom to feel him . . . Haven't you felt your father's influence and affinity in this way thousands of times from outer space where nothing, nothing,

S . . . , can ever be lost? Do not believe that anything that is part of our true realities could disappear or cease to exist: that which had so steadily worked its effects on us had already been a reality independent of all our present and familiar circumstances. This is precisely why we experienced it in such a different way and as responding to a completely independent need, because from the beginning it was aimed and determined at something beyond the here and now. All of our true relations, all of our penetrating experiences reach through the *Whole,* through life and death; *we have to live in Both, be intimately at home in both.* I know people who are already facing both the one and the other quite intimately and with the same love. And is life truly less mysterious and more familiar to us than that other condition? Are they not both placed namelessly above us, and equally out of reach. We are true and pure only in our willingness toward the whole, the undecided, the great, and the greatest.

Alas, only those can depart from us whom we never possessed. And we cannot even mourn this fact that we have never truly owned one person or another: we would have neither time nor strength nor justice to do so. For already the most fleeting experience of true possession (or of a commonality that is really just a double possession) casts us back into ourselves with such tremendous force, gives us so much to do there, demands of us to grow there in such intense solitude that it would be enough to keep us busy as individuals forever.

Now my attitude toward death is that it startles me more in those whom I have somehow failed to encounter and who remained unexplained or disastrous for me rather than in those whom I loved with certainty when they were alive, even if they had attained only a brief moment of radiance in the transfiguration of that intimacy that love can reach. With just a bit of innocence and pleasure taken in reality (which is entirely independent of time), it would never have occurred to people to think that they could ever again lose something to which they had truly attached themselves. No constellation of stars is as steadfast, no achievement as irrevocable as relations among humans that, beginning with the moment of their becoming visible, occur with far greater force in the realm of the invisible: in those depths where our existence is as permanent as gold lodged in rock, more lasting than a star.

Through loss, through great, immoderate loss, we are actually quite introduced into the *Whole*. Death is only an unsparing way of placing us on intimate and trusting terms with that side of our existence that is turned away from us. (What should I emphasize *more: our* or *existence*? Both are here of the greatest significance, as if balanced by the weight of all the stars!)

See, I think that now you are expected for the first time to suffer death itself in the death of an individual who is infinitely close to you, death in its entirety (somehow more than only your own possible death) that now has come the moment that you are most capable of apprehending the reality of the pure secret that, believe me, is not of death but of life.

The task now becomes to consider death in pain's ineffable and inexhaustible magnanimity, all of death since it has become available to you at the expense of something dear to you (and you have become related to it), as part of life, as something that can no longer be refused, no longer be denied. Pull it toward you with all your might, this dreadful thing, and as long as you cannot do that, at least *act* as if you are intimate with it. Do not scare it off by being scared of it (like everyone else). Interact with it, or, if that is still too much of an effort for you, at least hold still so that death's always chased-off essence can come very close and snuggle up to you. This, you see, is what death has become among us: something always chased away that could no longer allow itself to be recognized. If at the moment when it hurts and devastates us, death would be treated by one person, the least among us, with familiarity (and not with horror), with what kind of confessions would it—infinitely—yield to him! Only a brief moment of good intentions toward it, a short suppression of prejudice, and it will offer countless intimacies that would overwhelm our tendency to endure it in trembling hesitation.

.

Does our human state not obligate us to consent joyfully to everything that changes? And then, is this self-satisfied change truly of such significance? In this world, which takes pride in its speed and versatility, the principal values, even if they have been put to use badly, have lost neither their grandeur nor their danger. The few constants that make us gravitate remain intact and next to them the countless deviations seem quite useless. We ought to envision a world that is forever assured about these phenomena, which are not only contradictory but, moreover, only tenuously linked to each other.

.

It is the peculiar prerogative of our mourning that *there* where it does not appear distracted by the contradiction that in individual cases we consider a life to be apparently unfinished, interrupted, torn off—*there* mourning can be nothing but learning, nothing but achievement, the purest, most perfect coming to one's senses. And nowhere does this strange task become greater for us than when we are exposed to ourselves due to the loss of the father, in his high age, which then obligates us, as it were, to compose ourselves newly and to reach nothing less than a first independence of our inner ability.

As long as our father is alive for us, we are a kind of relief cast against him as background (hence the tragic dimension of our conflicts), and it is not until this blow that we become a whole sculpture in the round, free, alas, standing freely on all sides . . . (our mother, with her courage, had from the beginning placed us as far outside as she could).

•

Yes: the more a person has recognized here, the more farewells he will have had to accomplish over the course of his life. But I often feel as if all these partings would once again be affirmations in an open world where they would bear different names.

•

There is no task as urgent for us as to learn daily how to die, but our knowledge of death is not increased by the renunciation of life; only the ripe fruit of the here and now that has been seized and bitten into will spread its indescribable taste in us.

•

It is said either: that death is such an indescribable, immeasurable value that god permits it to be inflicted on us always even in the most senseless ways simply because there is nothing greater that he may bestow on us. Or that our personal existence has no significance for god, and, far from assigning it a duration, he knows nothing of it and of the tremendous value we attribute to how long it may last. There is no danger that this insight, if *truly* experienced just once, would result in causing freer minds to deny god, but it could delimit the essential conditions of his existence in relation to our own. There is nothing that renders us more incapable of truly experiencing god than our stubbornness in wanting to recognize his hand *in those places* where it has always been withheld—and by imagining his participation in so many things that matter to us, we probably overlook its signs and most glaring proofs while they become manifest elsewhere.

I have repeatedly read your letter in order to be close to you and to understand and grasp fully your current state of pain. How deep this pain must be since you were able to enter into its becalmed spots (few people, simply because of their suspicions about pain, reach those areas), and how real it is since you are able to track it into its most physical states and experience it in both of its extremes: entirely as psychic pain, where it exceeds us so immensely that we experience it only as silence, as a pause and interval of our nature, and then again, suddenly, at its other end, where it is like bodily suffering, a clumsy inconsolable child's pain that makes us moan. But is it not wonderful (and is this not somehow also an achievement of the maternal) to be thus led through the contrasts of one's being? And indeed you experience it often like a consecration and induction into the *Whole,* and as if nothing evil or deadly in a bad sense could ever befall us once we have purely and truly undergone this elementary suffering just once. I have often told myself that it was the compulsion or (if one may put it this way) the sacred cunning of martyrs that they demanded to be completely done with pain, the most terrible pain, excessive pain, which otherwise unpredictably spreads over and merges with the moments of one's life in smaller or larger doses of bodily and mental pain, that they demanded to conjure up and evoke *at once* the entire capacity for suffering so that after getting through it, there would be nothing but beatitude, the uninterrupted beatitude in beholding god, which will now remain undisturbed at the conclusion of these overcomings . . . The loss that has cast its shadow over you also presents a task of survival, and indeed a *reappraisal of* and *coming to terms with* all of the suffering that could befall us (for once the mother leaves us, all protection is gone); we are forced into a tremendous process of toughening up, but in return (and even *that* you were beginning to feel already) . . . in return the power to protect passes over to you, and all the gentleness that until now you had still been allowed to *receive* will increasingly come to blossom inside of you and it will now be *your* new capacity to distribute it, on your own initiative, as something of your own (something inherited and acquired beyond words and at the deepest expense).

I have already suggested to you several times how in both life and work I increasingly strive to correct all of our old repressions: those repressions that pushed beyond our reach and alienated us from the secrets that could replenish our lives with abundance. Life's dreadfulness has startled and horrified people, but where are the sweet and magnificent things that do not occasionally wear *this* mask, the mask of horror? Life itself—and we do not know anything besides it—is it not dreadful? Yet as soon as we admit its dreadfulness—not as an adversary, for *how* could we be its match?—but remain somehow filled with confidence that this very

dreadfulness belongs entirely to *us* and that it is at the present mo-
ment simply still too large, too expansive, too unembraceable for
our aspiring hearts . . . as soon as we affirm its most horrendous
dreadfulness at the risk of perishing of it (i.e., of the excess in our-
selves!), we gain an inkling of the most blissful state that can be
ours at this cost. Whoever does not at some point absolutely affirm
and even rejoice fully in the dreadfulness of life will never lay claim
to the inexpressible powers of our existence; he will pass through
life along the periphery and will have been, once the decision has
been cast, neither one of the living nor one of the dead.

To understand our *being here* as one side of being in its entirety and
to exhaust it passionately, this would be the demand placed on us
by death; while life, as long as one truly admits it, is in every spot
all of life.

How very much I hope that your worries will be laid to rest and
that you will emerge from them somewhat fortified: for truly, in
order to live we have to believe that every evil conceals a pure
blessing, which we in our blindness would have rebuffed had it
been offered to us without this painful disguise.

We are, one must consider, always equally close to death, only
without any tangible defense against it; while nature, in moments
of sudden alarm, lines up everything against death so that especially
when it struggles to distance itself from death by all means, we
seem to enter into a relation of proximity to death. In reality we
are, by the mere fact of life, so near it that we could not get closer
to it under any circumstances . . .

In life there is death and it astonishes me that everyone claims to ig-
nore this fact: there is death, the pitiless presence of which we are
made aware with every change that we survive because one must
learn to die slowly. We must learn how to die: there is all of life. To
prepare from afar the masterpiece of a proud and supreme death, of
a death where chance does not play a role, of a death that is well
wrought, quite happy, of an enthusiasm that the saints had known
how to achieve; the masterpiece of a long-ripened death that ef-
faces its odious name by restoring to the anonymous universe the
recognized and rescued laws of an intensely accomplished life.
During a long succession of experiences beginning in my child-
hood, this idea of death has painfully developed within me. It has
now become my inner mandate to suffer this small death with hu-
mility in order to become worthy of that event, which needs us to
be grand.

To understand the orbits of these small heart-stars [of animals]: this
is also an initiation into one's own life; and even if these cheerful
moons reflect for us the purest world-sun, it might have been al-
ways through the side that is always turned away from us that we
are placed in relation to the infinite life-space behind them.

Death is the *side of life* that is turned away from us and out of our
light's reach: we must try to achieve the greatest consciousness of
our existence that would be at home in *both of these unlimited realms*
and *inexhaustibly nourished by both*. The true gestalt of life extends
through *both* realms, the blood of the widest circulation pulses
through both: *there is neither a Here nor a Beyond but only the great
unity* where the beings that surpass us, the "angels," are at home.

.

Never has death remained as an obstacle in the life of a surviving individual, especially not the kind of death that had been suffered most deeply. Its innermost essence is not contrary to us, as one may sometimes surmise, but it is more knowledgeable about life than we are in our most vital moments. I always think that such a burden, with its immense pressure, is somehow meant to force us into a deeper and more interior layer of life so that we will grow out of it all the more fertile. Circumstances taught me this experience very early on and it has been confirmed for me from pain to pain: it is, finally, all that is *here* which is given to and expected of us, and we must try to transform every encounter into a new familiarity and friendliness with it. For where else should we turn with our senses that are so exquisitely equipped for grasping and mastering *this*—and how could we renounce our obligation to admire that which god has entrusted to us, since this surely contains all possible preparation for every future and eternal admiration!

.

The most profound experiences of my life have the cumulative effect of making me accept death as another part of this trajectory whose vertiginous curve we follow without being able to stop even for a moment. I find myself increasingly compelled to agree, in my provisional position, with this Everything where life and death incessantly penetrate and merge with each other. The angel of my affirmations (*der Engel des Jasagens*) turns a radiant face toward death. Although life requires so much else, it is above all *death* that has been weighed down by so much bad suspicion. For this reason I would like to rehabilitate it by placing it in that central spot, which it never left but from which all eyes have been averted. I consider it my task to demonstrate that death constitutes part of the wealth of this formidable Everything of which life is perhaps the tiniest part, even though it already surpasses our means and measures with such abundance. For this change in attitude to be completely accepted, we need as our premise events filled with constancy and permanence—and I too can state that I feel "so very much the same in spirit and in body," and that once I consent infinitely to the necessary transformations and to all of the good-byes imposed on us by the sovereign rhythm, I can see the fog of all these changes becoming transparent thanks to our flame, which passes through it without ever going out.

ON LANGUAGE

That Vast, Humming,

and Swinging Syntax

To be someone, as an artist, means: to be able to speak one's self. This would not be so difficult if language started with the individual, originated in him and would then, from this point, gradually force itself into the ears and the comprehension of others. But this is not the case. Quite on the contrary, language is what all have in common, but which no single person has produced because all are continuously producing it, that vast, humming, and swinging syntax to which everyone feels free to add by speaking what is closest to his heart. And then it happens that someone who is different from his neighbors on the inside loses himself by speaking himself out like the rain that is lost in the sea. For everything that is unique to an individual, if it does not wish to remain silent, needs its proper language . . . To say the same with the same words does not constitute progress.

In what soil of misery we poet-moles are digging around, never sure where we will push up and who might devour us at that very spot where we stick our dusty nose out of the soil.

There can be no question, none whatsoever, of making "helpful" books. The help must not be located *in* the book but at best in the relation between the reader and the book: there in this space that remains between the one who reads and the book (this peculiar space, which finds its equivalent in the imaginary space of painting and in the spatiality that surrounds and is governed by a sculpture) the misunderstanding of assistance might become a transparent event.

·

When writing poetry one is always assisted and even carried away by the rhythm of all things outside, for the lyric cadence is that of nature: of the waters, the wind, the night. But in order to shape prose rhythmically, one has to immerse oneself deeply within oneself and detect the blood's anonymous, multivaried rhythm. Prose is to be built like a cathedral: there one is truly without name, without ambition, without help: up in the scaffolding, alone with one's conscience.

·

What one writes at the age of twenty-one is nothing but screaming—and does anyone consider whether a scream ought to have been screamed differently? Language is still so thin for us in those years that the scream passes through it and carries with it only what clings to it. One will always develop in a way that makes one's language fuller, denser, firmer (heavier), and this of course makes sense only for someone who is sure that the scream in him also incessantly and inexorably gathers force so that later, compressed by countless atmospheres, it emerges evenly from all of the pores of the nearly impenetrable medium.

·

Increasingly, it seems to me a question of the right proportion whether something created out of one's heart and soul belongs in the public sphere at all. We certainly ought not to take lightly anything that is truthful and gives untainted testimony of itself, and yet to everything with such effects there corresponds a particular force field. The world's anarchy is perhaps caused by nothing more grievously than by the near-complete loss of insight into the measure and commensurability of works with such effects. The forces that would gather into the center of a considerable radius, if only they were left alone, find themselves flung out into the open where they instantly lose all proportionality. The squandering of such forces has never been worse and more nonsensical, and even carefully circumscribed areas everywhere become impoverished while outlying space gains nothing from receiving the tensions appropriated from them. It is by now a hereditary misunderstanding that anyone, as long as no simple communication is concerned, could "publish" a certain embodiment of the spirit. Every such thing forms the center of either a smaller or a greater sphere, and while it is unlikely that something that by its nature has the attributes and relations of the stars could be kept private and unique to oneself for long, the strength and radiance of something else is certainly not heightened by exposing it and tearing down the walls around it. A world that has dissolved into publicity will have to submit to this correction as its most essential change: to return every force to its corresponding sphere. The overall objective would be the expropriation of all individual forces, which would of course entail the suspension of what we currently call art and spirit, along with all of the soul's interiority and the arrangements in one's heart.

•

There is so much more reality in a successful poem than in any personal relation or affection I may feel; wherever I create I am real and I want to find the strength to base my entire life on this truth, on this boundless simplicity and joy that is occasionally given to me.

I suppose that just as in poetry, in politics purely human, deliberately human intentions do not count for very much. Poetry that *wants to* console, to help, or to lend support to whatever noble conviction would be a kind of weakness that might be moving at times . . . But what matters is not a charitable and tender intention but one's submission to an authoritarian dictation that *wants* neither good nor bad (of which we know so little) and instead quite simply compels us to arrange our sentiments, our ideas, and the entire upheaval of our existence in accordance with that greater order, which exceeds us to a degree that it could never become an object of our comprehension . . . My reproach to "freedom" is that it leads man at best to a point that he still understands, but never any further. Freedom by itself does not suffice; even when employed deliberately and justly, it leaves us halfway, on the narrow lot of our reason.

It is frightening to think how many things are made and unmade with words; they are so far removed from us, trapped in their eternal imprecision, indifferent with regard to our most urgent needs; they recoil at the moment when we seize them; they have their life and we have ours.

It is contrary to nature to part with books with which one agrees, just as it is important in the same case not to hold on to people for too long.

Do not say anything against rhyme! It is a mighty goddess indeed, the deity of very secret and very ancient coincidences, and one must never let the fires on its altars burn out. She is extremely temperamental: one can neither anticipate nor invoke her. She arrives like happiness itself, her hands filled with blossoms of fulfillment. [. . .] True rhyme is not a means of poetry but an infinitely affirming "yes" that the gods impress like a seal on our most innocent emotions.

•

To be honest with you, the longer I live, the more difficult it becomes for me to find an immediate, valid response to words like those sent by you. And it is not only that it becomes more difficult, I also make it harder on myself by asking where finally I might find confirmation in attempting such a response at all. Whatever success and insight fortuitously come together in my poem or in another work of art is not the same as the mastery and the achievement of daily life—and if it were a matter of deciding which one of us is more worthless, my side would perhaps outweigh yours. In spite of all of his difficulties, the creative and productive person of course finds confirmation in that great force which occasionally makes use of him and which then achieves so much with him that no matter how embattled he might otherwise feel he musters the patience to endure for its sake. How others who are engulfed by suffering might reach the deep and fertile ground for forbearance: I have often wondered about that, without having reached an explanation. But we have to admit that hardly anything exists that is offered to our view in such varied manifestations, ranging from banal examples to unforgettable formations, as this fact: that life has been achieved in the most insulting, grueling, and even deadliest circumstances and that individuals were capable of loving life when it was altogether horrific. And even that individuals who had long endured a radiant fate indifferently, without much pleasure or engagement, had unfolded their heart's joyousness and security when suddenly their situation plunged into despair, and they found themselves sick, abused, at the bottom of unfathomable prisons; and that they began to know and were first entitled to truly relish their heart's capacities only upon reaching such a state. I have traced the stories of such lives wherever I could with great enthusiasm, and although I could not make out a glimpse of the *secret* that makes such tremendous survivals possible, I nonetheless live in the conviction *that* they occur all the time.

·

At bottom one searches in everything new (country or person or thing) only for an expression that will aid one's personal confessions to reach greater force and maturity. All things exist in order to become images for us in some sense. And this does not cause them any harm: for while they express us ever more clearly, our soul bows down to them to the same degree.

·

This, indeed, is life's most fervent miracle: to suspend us in a state of hovering from which we may still impart something but can no longer reveal ourselves . . .

ON ART

Art Presents Itself as a

Way of Life

The creations of art always result from a state of having-been-in-danger, from an experience of having-gone-to-the-end, up to the point where no human can go any further. The further one ventures, the more proper, the more personal, the more singular an experience becomes—finally, the art object is the necessary, irrepressible, most definitive expression of this singularity . . . In this way the art object can be of such tremendous help in the life of the one compelled to create it—it is his summary: the knot in the rosary at which his life says a prayer, the ever recurring proof of his unity and truthfulness that is given to no one but himself and whose outward effects appear anonymous, nameless, as nothing but necessity, as reality, as existence.

.

The work of art is adjustment, balance, reassurance. It can be neither gloomy nor full of rosy hopes for its essence consists of justice.

.

Art presents itself as a way of life, not unlike religion, science, and socialism. It differs from these other modes of understanding only in that it is not a product of its time and appears, as it were, as the worldview of the ultimate goal.

.

Asceticism, of course, is no solution: it is sensuality with a negative prefix. For a saint this might become useful, as a kind of scaffolding. At the intersection of his various acts of renunciation he beholds that god of opposition, the god of the invisible who has not yet created anything. But anyone who has committed to using his senses in order to grasp appearances as pure and forms as true on earth: how could such an individual even begin to distance himself from anything! And even if such renunciation proved initially helpful and necessary for him, in his case it would be nothing more than a deception, a ruse, a scheme—and ultimately it would take its revenge somewhere in the contours of his finished work by showing up there as an undue hardness, aridity, barrenness, and cowardice.

•

Art is childhood, after all. Art means to be oblivious to the fact that the world already *exists* and to create one. Not to destroy what one encounters but simply not to find anything complete. Countless possibilities. Countless wishes. And suddenly to be fulfillment, to be summer, to have sun. Without speaking about it, unwittingly. Never to be done. Never to have the seventh day. Never to see that all is good. Dissatisfaction is youth. God was too old at the beginning, I think. Otherwise he would not have stopped on the evening of the sixth day. And not on the thousandth day. Still not today. This is all I hold against him. That he could expend himself. That he thought that his book was finished with the creation of the human and that he has now put away his quill to wait and see how many editions will be printed. That he was no artist is so very sad. That *yet* he was no artist. One wants to cry over this and lose all courage for everything.

•

The life of any man who has reached a certain level in his engagement with art is disfigured in ways that from a certain angle appear close to mania. So much temerity is needed in art that outside of it the artist often displays a ridiculous kind of cowardice; it's that his courage . . . (I have preferred to express this in the following way: "It is true, I am 'chicken'—but for this reason I am sometimes allowed to crow as a rooster, too!")

•

What I write as an artist will always retain the traces of contradiction with which I began myself, and yet, if you ask me, I do not want *this* to be the principal effect of these works: young people ought not to read these texts as invitations for rebellion and liberation nor for the abandonment of the tasks imposed on them by their time. Rather that they would accept with a new sense of agreement what is given, forced upon us, necessary in some circumstances, and that they would not so much resist the pressure of their circumstances but instead exploit it by letting it push them into a denser, deeper, and more authentic layer of their own nature.

If I speak like this today and thus endorse acceptance, agreement, and endurance (which I myself failed to achieve), then this (here I am strict with myself) is not the older man's softness speaking—but the times have changed indeed. Between that most difficult decade of my childhood and the current (even the most awful) attitude there is a difference that can hardly be measured; even if the abyss between father and son is being torn open every day anew, certain agreements are possible across it and have even become so commonplace that we don't notice them anymore.

•

We most certainly need to test ourselves against the most extreme possibilities, just as we are probably obligated not to express, share, and impart this most extreme possibility *before* it has entered the work of art. As something unique that no other person would and should understand, as one's personal madness, so to speak, it has to enter into the work to attain its validity and to reveal there an internal law, like primary patterns that become visible only in the transparency of artistic creation. There exist nonetheless two freedoms to express oneself that seem to me the ultimate possibilities: one in the presence of the created object, and the other within one's actual daily life where one can show another person what one has become through work, and where one may in this way mutually support and help and (here understood humbly) admire one another. In either case, however, it is necessary to show results, and it is neither lack of confidence nor lack of intimacy nor a gesture of exclusion if one does not reveal the tools of one's personal becoming that are marked by so many confusing and torturous traits, which are valid only for one's own use.

As much as the artist within one directs his intention toward the *work,* its realization, its existence and duration, beyond us—one is truly just with regard to art only when even this most urgent realization of a higher visibility, setting out from an ultimately extreme perspective, is recognized as nothing but the means to recapture something entirely invisible, wholly interior and possibly inconspicuous: a healthier and more integrated state at the center of one's own being.

So much has been written (both well and poorly) about things that the things themselves no longer hold an opinion but appear only to mark the imaginary point of intersection for certain clever theories. Whoever wants to say anything about them speaks in reality only about the views of his predecessors and lapses into a semipolemical spirit that stands in exact opposition to the naïve productive spirit with which each object wants to be grasped and understood.

·

It is always forgotten that the philosopher, just like the poet, is the carrier of futures among us, and that he may therefore not count as strongly on the support of his time. Philosophers and poets are contemporaries of the people in the far-off future, and as soon as they are done with agitating the neighbors they have no reason to reach order or draw conclusions in their development, aside from those systematic compilations that they need in order to survey their own situation but that they destroy again as quickly to advance their internal progress. Once his achievement has been systematized and expressed in words, once students, disciples, and friends rally around it and enemies attack it, then the philosopher has lost the right to rattle the foundation of this now inhabited system and jeopardize the thousands of individuals whose livelihood now depends on it. He has impeded his own ruthless progress, which perhaps could arise only from the ruins of this order, and while only yesterday he had still been unlimited master of thousands of developments, who could indulge every nuance of his will in a king's fashion, he has now become the highest servant of a system that grows larger than its founder with each passing day. Philosophers should be patient and wait and not harbor wishes to reign over an empire supported by the means of its time. They are the kings of what is yet to come, and their crowns are still one with the ore buried in the veins of our mountains . . .

The fact is that the most progressive individuals bestow things on the future and consequently have to be stern in their dealings with the present. They don't have any bread to offer the hungry—no matter how often they themselves may think so . . . they have stones that their contemporaries mistake for bread and nourishment but that at bottom will lie as the foundations for future days, which they must not give away. Consider the infinite freedom of the individual who is without fame and unknown; *this* is the kind of freedom the philosopher must guard for himself: that every day he may be someone new, a *refuter of himself.*

I consider art to be the individual's effort to come to an agreement with all things beyond the narrow and obscure, with the smallest as well as the largest, and to further approach in such consistent dialogues all of life's ultimate, quiet sources. The secrets of things fuse inside this individual with his most profound sensations and become audible for him, as if they were his proper longings. The rich language of these intimate confessions is what we call beauty.

An art object is ruthless and has to be that way.

One is tempted to explain the work of art in this way: as a profoundly interior confession that is released under the pretext of a memory, an experience, or an event, and that can exist on its own when thus detached from its creator. This independence of the work of art is what is called beauty. With every work of art a new thing is added to the world. You will find that this definition accommodates everything: from the Gothic cathedrals of

Jehan de Beauce [French mason, fifteenth/sixteenth century] to a piece of furniture by the young van de Velde [Belgian craftsman, nineteenth/twentieth century].

Don't wait for me to tell you about my inner state—I have to keep quiet about it; it would be bothersome even just for myself to account for all of the changes in fortune to which I had to submit in my struggle to reach a state of concentration. This reversal of all one's strengths, this change of direction of the soul never takes place without a series of crises. Most artists avoid these by taking recourse to various distractions. But it is for the same reason that they never again succeed in reaching the center of their creativity from which they had set out at the moment of their purest momentum. Each time at the beginning of work one must re-create this initial innocence and return to this naïve state where the angel had revealed itself to you and imparted its first welcome. One must then search behind the brambles for the bed where one had fallen asleep. Only this time one will not sleep there, one will beg and moan, it doesn't matter; if then the angel deigns to reappear, it is because you have persuaded him not with tears but with your humble decision to always begin again: *to be a novice!*

As an artist you should not believe that you will be tested in your work. You are not who you claim to be and whom one or another might take you for because he doesn't know any better, as long as work has not become your nature to such a degree that you *cannot* do otherwise but prove yourself in it. Working in this way, you are the expertly cast javelin: laws are imparted to you from the thrower's hand and reach the target at the same time with you. What could be more secure than your flight?

Your test, however, shall be that you will not always be thrown. That you will not be chosen by the javelin-thrower named loneliness for a long time, that she will forget you. This is the time of temptations when you feel unused, unable. (As if it would not keep you busy enough simply to be prepared!) Then, when you are resting there with not much weight, all kinds of distractions try their hand with you and want to find out how else you want to be used. As a blind man's staff, as one of the bars in a railing, or as a ropewalker's balancing rod. Or they are quite capable of planting you in the soil of fate so that the miracle of the seasons would happen to you, and you would perhaps sprout little green leaves of happiness . . .

•

I have often told myself that art, as I conceive of it, is a movement against nature. God had surely never anticipated that any one of us would perform this terrible turning back on the self, which ought to be permitted only to the saint who claims to besiege his god by attacking from an unforeseen and poorly defended side. But we who are not saints, from where do we approach ourselves when we turn our back on what is happening, on our future—and even, in order to cast ourselves into that abyss of our being that swallows us up, without the kind of confidence that takes us there and that seems stronger than the gravitational pull of our own nature? If it is the meaning of sacrifice that the moment of the greatest danger coincides with the instant when one is saved, then certainly nothing resembles sacrifice more than this terrible will to art. How stubborn and insane it is! Everything that others forget in order to make life possible we constantly strive to uncover and even make bigger; we actually awaken our monsters that we then do not oppose sufficiently to be able to slay them. Because in a certain sense we find ourselves in agreement with them; these monsters, after all, possess this surplus of power that is indispensable to those who feel compelled to exceed themselves. Unless one wants to understand this act of victory as more mysterious and much more profound, it is not our role to consider ourselves the tamers of our inner lions. But suddenly we find ourselves marching alongside them as if in a triumphal procession without being able to recall so much as the instant of this inconceivable reconciliation (an ever-so-slightly sloped bridge links what is terrible to what is gentle).

.

Even when music speaks, it still does not speak to us. The perfectly created work of art concerns us only *insofar* as it survives us. The poem enters from the inside into language, from a dimension that is always turned away from us; it fills language wonderfully and wells up within it to its rim—but from that point on it is beyond our reach. Colors find expression in a painting, but they are worked into it like rain into the landscape; and the sculptor teaches the stone nothing but how to shut in on itself most magnificently. Music, of course, is still close to us in its essence: it rushes toward us and we block its path so it passes straight through us. Music is almost like the air of higher regions: we breathe it deeply into the lungs of our spirit, and it infuses a more expansive blood into our hidden circulation. Yet *how far* music reaches beyond us! Yet *how far* it pushes on with no regard for us! Yet *how much* of which it carries right through us we still fail to seize! Alas, we fail to seize it, alas, we lose it.

.

In art, if one has time to persevere and to create a whole work that is not interrupted anywhere, all oppositions, even conceptual ones, are necessary and can finally amount to an alternating rhythm.

•

Who among us would not have to strive for *this* above everything else: to reach such security in one's ability that one has always the correct counterweights ready within one's conscience to offset the judgment that arrives from the outside.

•

[I]f there is no art that was not religious in its beginnings, it nonetheless still holds true in all cases that it reconstituted the nearly forgotten, long completed god in images painted from a memory which had not yet grown cold. And pious artists might have preserved this memory, like the mother of a child who passed away two or three days after birth and for whom the sweetness of emotional possession enigmatically fuses with her pain to yield a rare feeling that seems to encompass all of the sensations possible in the world.

•

An individual who has committed himself to art and now wrestles within it, having given up everything else, has also become strict, you see. Such a person is more likely to warn off others rather than to beckon them to enter into a realm of the most tremendous demands and indescribable sacrifices. And for someone sitting at his desk, behind closed doors, matters are still relatively simple: at least he has to deal only with himself. But an actor, even when his work originates in the purest exigencies of his being, stands in the open and performs his work in the open where he is exposed to all the influences, detractions, disturbances, and even hostilities that originate in his colleagues and his audience and that interrupt, distract, and split him off. For him things are more difficult than for anyone else; above all, he needs to lure success and to base his actions on it. And yet what misery results if this new alignment leads him to abandon the inner direction that had driven him into art in the first place. He seems to have no self; his job consists in letting others dictate selves to him. And the audience, once it has accepted him, wants to preserve him within the limits where it finds entertainment; and yet his achievement depends entirely upon his capacity to maintain an interior constancy through all kinds of changes, blindly, like a madman. Any momentary weakness toward success is as sure to doom him as giving in and drawing on applause as a precondition for their creation spells doom for the painter or poet.

Just as a puppy dog strives to become nothing but simply a dog and as thoroughly a dog as possible, one has to grow into art as the mode of existence for which one's heart and lungs were made, as the only appropriate option. If one chances upon art from the outside, it ends up being nothing but a bad disguise, and life, in its unshakable honesty, takes it upon itself to tear off this masquerade.

For most people, the game of consent and refusal where much can be lost and much can be gained constitutes the principal and welcome way of passing time throughout their lives. The artist belongs to those who have renounced all gains and losses with a single, irreversible expression of consent: for neither gain nor loss exists any longer in the realm of law, in the realm of pure obedience.

This definitive, free affirmation of the world shifts the heart to another plane of experience. The balls cast to elect this experience are no longer called happiness and unhappiness; its poles are not marked as life and death. Its measure is not the distance between opposites.

Who still thinks that art constitutes the beautiful which has an opposite (this little "beautiful" that has its origins in the concept of taste)? Art is the passion toward the whole. Its result: equanimity and the balance of completeness.

·

I cannot even imagine the individual arts sufficiently distinct from one another. This admittedly exaggerated attitude might have its most acute origin in the fact that in my youth, I, quite inclined toward painting, had to decide in favor of another art so as not to be distracted. And thus I made this decision with a certain passionate exclusivity. Based on my experience, incidentally, every artist needs to consider for the sake of intensity *his* means of expression to be basically the *only one possible* while he is producing. For otherwise he could easily suspect that this or that piece of world would not be expressible by *his* means at all and he would finally fall into that most interior gap *between* the individual arts, which is surely wide enough and could be genuinely bridged only by the vital tension of the great Renaissance masters. *We* are faced with the task of deciding purely, each one alone, on his *one* mode of expression, and for each creation that is meant to be achieved *in this one area* all support from the other arts is a weakening and a threat.

·

Freedom should be recommended only to someone who knows what boundless responsibility is. At the bottom of art, there are no more rules that could be transcribed, but there occur moments when the purest laws become manifest for the individual who submits to it in an ultimate sense!

·

The question whether art is to be experienced as a great forgetting or as a greater insight perhaps only appears to have an unambiguous answer. One could imagine that both points are valid: that a certain kind of surrender, which comes close to forgetting, could constitute the preliminary stage for new insights or a kind of transfer to a higher plane of life where there would commence a more mature, greater seeing, a looking with rested, fresh eyes. To stay with forgetting, of course, would be most incorrect. I believe that when confronted with those arts that appear with overwhelming force (music, for instance), a lot of people simply surrender comfortably to it. This (I fear) may be what the majority understands quite properly as the "enjoyment" of art: a sluggishness at the expense of the abundances that are operative in a work of art. This is also where the quaint misunderstanding of the bourgeois sets in who instantly begins to relax wherever he sees that more has been accomplished than what he understands. Ultimately, it will be a matter of one's spiritual conscience how far one permits oneself to drown in an artistic impression or whether one may have to keep one's eyes open while persisting in it. Music has often been capable of bringing me simple "oblivion." But the more receptive I have grown, frequently on arduous paths with the help of images, imagistic works, and books, the more prepared I have also become in my response to music, and the less music succeeds in flooding me entirely and making me feign a transformation where, after all, I could not maintain myself beyond the moment of its occurrence.

Artistic work is fraught with many dangers, and in individual cases it is often not clearly discernible whether in a particular instance one advances or is driven back by the onslaught of excessive forces with which one has become involved. In such cases it is necessary to wait and to endure. For me this has always proven very difficult since I neglect everything else when I am working, so that during such interludes I lack everything including the site where one could wait out such a decision. Probably never more than in the past year have I viewed with greater passion those people who are engaged in good and balanced activities, something that one "can" always do, something that depends more upon intelligence, reflection, insight, experience—who knows what—than on those tremendous tensions of one's interior life that no one can control. These are no exaltations, surely not, for then they could not result in something so indescribably real in the spiritual realm. But their impact and rebound are so incommensurate with any scale that one would think our heart incapable of enduring such extreme oscillations toward either side.

.

I have noticed to what a great degree art is a matter of conscience. Nothing is needed as urgently in artistic work as one's conscience: that is the only measure. (Critique does not provide a measure, and even the approval or rejection by others that takes place outside of critical commentary may only very rarely become an influence, and then only under very carefully established conditions.) It is, therefore, quite important not to abuse one's conscience in those early years and not to become callous at the spot on which it rests. It has to remain light in all of this; one must have as little awareness of it as of some interior organ out of our will's reach. But even the slightest pressure exerted by it must be taken into account. For otherwise, the scale that will later have to weigh every future word of verse loses its extreme nimbleness.

.

The practice of artistic seeing first had to overcome itself to the point where even in the midst of what is terrible and apparently repulsive, it beholds only being that is *valid* along with everything else that is. Just as the artist may not choose what he wants to behold, he may not turn his gaze away from any form of existence. A single instance of refusal exiles him from the state of grace, and he becomes utterly sinful.

This act of lying-down-with-the-leper and sharing all-of-one's-warmth, including the heat of one's own heart during a night of love: all of this must have been part of the artist's life as an act of overcoming to reach his new state of beatitude. Behind this kind of devotion holiness begins with small things first: the simple life of a love that has persisted and that has joined itself to everything alone, inconspicuously, and wordlessly without taking any pride in it.

.

The "only work," as you put it, this inner wrestling aimed in the direction of god, does not have to suffer or vanish because we apply our strengths in what seem to be more superficial efforts. Don't forget that during times when craftsmanship was still filled with the warmth of life, for instance, nearly all of its rhythms and repetitions caused god to grow within those simple hearts; indeed, the incomparable advantage of being human may manifest itself most thoroughly where a person succeeds in introducing into something small and mundane the unseen vastness that governs his existence. The heap of confusions that complicate the transparency and order of our present existence has been dangerously enlarged by the fact that the appeals of art have so frequently been understood as a summons *to* art. Thus the manifestations of artistic creation—poems, paintings, sculptures, and the hovering creations of music—have recruited more and more young and promising people out of life instead of achieving their effects in life. This misunderstanding deprives life of many elements belonging to it, and the sphere of art where finally only a few great individuals achieve the right to last gets crowded with those who have been seduced and have taken refuge there. The poem means nothing less than to rouse the possible poet within its reader . . . , and the perfectly achieved painting says this above anything else: See, you don't have to paint; I am already here!

So at last we should reach complete agreement on *this* point: that art finally does not intend to appoint more artists. It does not mean to recruit anyone, and it remains always my suspicion that art pays no attention whatsoever to its effects. But when its creations, after having irrepressibly emerged from their inexhaustible origin, stand strangely still and superior among all other things, it could happen that they somehow become exemplary for *all* human activity through their innate selflessness, freedom, and intensity.

.

Quite early on, I already sensed that it was in the nature of certain mental creations to not feel sufficiently secured within and near us; then it is, so to speak, their own propulsion that lifts them into a higher or different sphere where they have a chance of lasting for a while independently of our transience. I am increasingly preoccupied with considering how pure this duration of the artwork may be since such a work generates its own space out of itself, and this space seems only superficially identical with the public spaciousness, which of course claims to have taken possession of this new thing.

.

The deeply moving artworks by unknown artists which have survived certainly lose neither power nor presence by our failure to link them to the fate or dates of their creators. As far as those are concerned who see themselves confronted with an artwork whose creator is still present or at least can still be traced, they are dealt far too cheap a favor when the creator's identity is explained to them. The indiscreet publicity of our era has at its disposal all kinds of machinery to seize and assess the artist behind his pretext, and artists themselves have accommodated and even preempted in every possible way the most violently intrusive curiosity . . .

                    •

It seems to me that for all those who are still in the process of becoming, the danger that results from being constantly exposed in the act of artistic creation has not been sufficiently recognized. Or possibly (to put this facetiously), people *want* this danger so that this superfluous profession can be dealt with once and for all. In the context of such revelations the situation of the work of art grows increasingly problematic. The audience has long forgotten that the work of art is not an object offered to them but one that has been placed purely into an imaginary realm where it exists and persists, and that this realm of its being only seems to be identical with the public sphere of transactions and trade. The artist's vanity, in combination with his softness and weakness in believing that he conveys immediate assistance and healing powers to the needy, has led him to unceasingly reinforce and complicate the audience's erroneous assumptions. The greatest and indeed most urgent task for any serious investigation into art seems to me to restore for the work of art its particular, indescribable situation, which in former times had been an easier task owing to the natural occurrence of timeless, blank spots reserved for the divine.

                    •

It is possible in art to stay always with "what one already knows," and by staying within that sphere of knowledge and experience, it expands and always again leads beyond the self. The "ultimate premonitions and insights" become reachable only for the individual who resides in and remains at work, and whoever contemplates them from a distance will not gain control over them. But all of this already belongs so much to the area of personal solutions. At bottom it is none of our business how someone manages to grow, if only he grows and if only we seek to determine the law of our own growth . . .

•

As soon as an artist has located the vital center of his activities, nothing will be more important for him than to remain within this center and never move further away from it (which is, of course, also the center of his nature, of his world) than to the interior walls of his quietly and steadily expanding achievement. His place is not, *never*, not even for a moment, next to the beholder and critic (at least no longer in an environment where all that is visible becomes ambiguous and preliminary, an auxiliary construction and temporary scaffolding for something else). And one basically needs to be an acrobat to leap back safely and unharmed from this point of view into one's inner center (the distances are too great and all the spots too destabilized to risk such an eminently inquisitive feat). Most artists today use up their strength in this back-and-forth, and in addition to wasting their energy they get terribly confused and lose a part of their essential innocence to the sin of having taken their work from the outside by surprise, to have tasted it, to have joined others in enjoying it!

•

It seems that all of this could be improved by assuming the stance about which I had written recently and that it is probably possible for us to reach since it might be nothing more than attentiveness. A little while ago, I put this to the test at the Louvre. I had been there several times, and on those occasions it had been as if I were facing uninterrupted action: things kept on happening and happening right before my eyes. And then, recently, there had been only images and too many images and just about everywhere someone was standing, and everything was a distraction. And I asked myself why it was different today. Was I tired? Yes. But of what did this fatigue consist? It consisted of my willingness to think of just about anything; it consisted of the passing of all kinds of things through me like water through a reflecting surface and of the dissolving of my contours into something flowing. And I told myself: I no longer want to be the reflecting image but that which hovers above it. And I turned myself in such a way so that I no longer stood on my head and for a brief instant I closed my eyes and pulled myself together and tightened my contours the way violin strings are tightened until you feel them taut and resounding, and suddenly I knew myself entirely within my outline like a drawing by [Albrecht] Dürer, and thus I stepped before the *Madonna Lisa:* and she was without equal. Do you see . . . So this is what one ought to be capable of at some point. Not to wait (which is what has been happening until now) for powerful things and good days to turn you into something but to preempt them and to be it yourself already: this is what one ought to be capable of at some point. Will then not everything be work? For what would be unproductive in this condition? There is delicious black soil within us, and our blood needs to move only like the plow and trace furrows. And then, while we are harvesting, somewhere else the seeding has already begun anew . . .

·

What is so terrible about art is that the further one advances in it, the more tightly one is committed to an extreme and nearly impossible objective. At this point one achieves mentally what the woman in one of [Charles] Baudelaire's poems means in another sense when she suddenly bursts out in the great silence of a moonlit night: *Que c'est un dur métier que d'être belle femme* [It's a tough job to be a beautiful woman].

•

Art is not to be understood as a *selection* made of the world but as its entire transformation into magnificence. The admiration with which art hurls itself upon things (everything without exception) ought to be so impetuous, so forceful, and so radiant that the object has no time to recall its ugliness or depravity. There can be nothing so off-putting and negating within terror that the multiple action of artistic mastery would not leave it with a great and positive surplus in the form of something expressing existence, desiring being: in the form of an angel.

•

A thing is definite; the art object has to be even more definite; removed from all chance, freed of all uncertainty, lifted out of time and given to space, it has become lasting, capable of eternity. The model *seems;* the art-thing *is.* In this way the one constitutes nameless progress over and beyond the other, the silent and growing realization of the desire to be, which emanates from everything in nature. This also rules out the erroneous assumption which tried to designate art as the most arbitrary and vain profession; it is the most humble service and supported entirely by law.

•

Look: I also do not wish to tear art and life apart violently: I know that sometime and somewhere, they are of one mind. But I am awkward in life, and for that reason, whenever life tightens around me, it often results in a moment of stasis, a delay that causes me to lose quite a lot, just as in a dream where one cannot finish getting dressed and misses over two stubborn buttons on a shoe an important event that will never return. And this is quite true, that life moves on and actually leaves no time for delays and many losses, especially for someone who wishes to have art. For art is a thing that is much too great and difficult and long for a life, and those of very advanced age are nothing but beginners in it. "It was not until the age of seventy-three that I understood approximately the form and true nature of birds, fishes, and plants," Hokusai has written, and Rodin felt the same way, and one might also consider Leonardo [da Vinci], who grew very old. And they have always lived in their art and, gathering themselves around it alone, they have allowed everything else to become overgrown. But how are you supposed to be unafraid when you only rarely reach your sanctuary, get trapped outside in life rising up, and knock yourself numb against all of its obstacles? This is why I long so impatiently to get to work, to begin my workday, because life can become art only once it has become work. I know that I cannot extricate my life from the fates with which it has grown intertwined, but I have to find the strength to lift life in its entirety, exactly the way it is and including everything, into calmness, into solitude, into the quiet of profound days of labor.

•

This is the basis for all artistic creation: to keep alert one's innermost conscience that lets us know for every expressed experience whether in this form it may be completely justified in its truthfulness and integrity. And this foundation would have to be created even when one's inspiration hovers in a state of suspension and is in no need, as it were, of any solid ground.

•

All creative activities, even of the most productive kind, serve finally only to establish a certain inner constancy. Perhaps art amounts to so much only because some of its purer creations guarantee the achievement of a more dependable inner adjustment (and so much more!). Especially in our era, when most people are driven by ambition to produce art (or what passes for art), one cannot insist too much on this ultimate and exclusive basis for judging art, which is so profound and secret that the most inconspicuous service toward achieving it deserves all the more to be considered on the same level with this most conspicuous and best known (actual production).

·

The way in which the artist who is denied his proper place in our era (which at most exploits and abuses him) is forced to become, depending upon his inclinations, either someone who conceals or who imposes himself amounts to such a general and obvious fate that the creative individual himself is to be blamed only for a minuscule fraction of this disaster. Now please understand me correctly: if I reproach our times with not having any genuine space and pure need for the artist, then this charge is made without any reproach against these times in which we live. There is nothing more futile and more absurd than to suspect and condemn the conditions of this present time, which constitute, determine, and move each one of us at every given moment. The present is ours and we belong to it, whether we want to or not, and only through it and by its means might we (occasionally) go beyond it. Nonetheless, it must be permitted to point out that today it is difficult for certain activities to gain a foothold and that the artistic will, which might arise in one of our contemporaries, seems particularly endangered, though far less by counterforces and contradictions than by the principal threat of an excess of manifold and confused desires, which want to use art to relieve our disappointments and calm our curiosity.

*

Our time is neither more distinguished nor lesser than any other. I have no intention of chastising it but only of describing it accurately when I suspect that it does not know how to employ the strengths that it has at its disposal: it alternately despises and boasts of them instead of putting them to use. Like every present it is also jealous of the future, and wherever something that is about to happen arises, it employs two successive steps in order to neutralize it: as long as this is feasible, it opposes the new but then adopts it quite suddenly, should it still persist, as if it were a minor in need of guidance. Thus it revokes, as it were, every prophet, first by contradicting him and then (more indirectly) by creating disciples: there exists no savior who will not be tempted by this fate.

*

For an object to become art, it must have a *higher* degree of inner oscillation which, owing to its nature, exceeds that of objects in daily usage or expressions in daily conversation. And a secondary effect of this oscillation is the intention to establish for this new creation, which exceeds all that is transient and—to put it plainly— private, a situation in which it could persist and survive longer and as something more open to the world. There can be no talk of "effect" here, not even with regard to the creation's actual exposure, which is only an accidental occurrence for a phenomenon that is of itself born into greater contexts. Whatever you may create with this attitude, within or next to or in spite of whatever profession you choose, you will always be justified in transcribing it, whether or not anyone sees or knows it—every word that is created in this way will help you and, beyond that, tell you one day where it belongs.

.

The things that are animate, part of our experience, and that seem *aware of our knowledge of them* are vanishing and can no longer be replaced. *We might be the last who will still have known such things.* And with us rests the responsibility not only to preserve *their* memory (that would be little and unreliable) but their human and laric worth ("laric" in the sense of the deities of the home).

.

Art always promises the most distant and then even more remote future, and for this reason the crowd that passionately reaches for the nearest future will always be of an iconoclastic bent. From an inexperienced and agitated perspective, the power of what is entirely in the future bafflingly resembles the authority of the past!

.

Revolution would mean for me the simple and pure legitimation of man and of the work that he likes to do and does well. Every program that does not place *this* goal as its end seems as pointless and perspectiveless to me as any of the previous governments and regimes . . .

.

A sense of security outside of that which is found in the poem, the painting, the equation, the building, the piece of music might be reached perhaps only at the cost of the most decisive delimitation. A sense of security may be thus established by enclosing oneself and settling within a considered or experienced segment of world, in an environment of familiarity and signification within which an immediate use of the self becomes necessary and possible. But how could we desire this? Our security must somehow become our relation to the whole, to completeness; to be secure means for us to become aware of the innocence of injustice and to admit the phenomenal reality of suffering. It means to reject names in order to honor behind them the only instantiations and relations of fate like guests. It means to remain steadfast with regard to food and deprivation, deep into the realm of the spiritual, as with regard to bread and stone; it means not to suspect anything, not to exclude it, and to consider nothing as an other; it means to live beyond any concept of property by relying on appropriations (not proprietary ones, but allegorical ones). And finally, although this does not apply to a bourgeois existence, to make oneself understood with regard to this audacious security: it is after all the final, foundational commonality of our rises and declines. To conceive of insecurity in the greatest terms—within infinite insecurity security also becomes infinite . . .

·

There truly is a difference between art as a way of life for someone or simply something they do. The first option is so immense, so slow, and perhaps so strictly limited to people of an advanced age that you have no reason to compare yourself to the individuals bearing this strange name. Only the truly great *are* artists in that strict but exclusively true sense that art has become a way of life for them—all others, all of us for whom art is still only something we do, encounter each other on the same long path and greet one another in the same silent hope while longing for the same remote mastery.

*

The confusion surrounding all artistic creation would be complete if a creative person were expected to temper and tame all of the demons he rouses at any given moment or if that work of art that offered the most useful and most immediate assistance were considered most pure. Let us be quite specific: the artist is someone afflicted with an inner mission who attempts to achieve *within* himself, under conditions that can never be repeated, an order that often remains incomprehensible in human terms because it is meant in terms of the world. As the clandestine and ruthless condensation of this process, the work of art is far from providing a remedy; instead it is its nature to unsettle and cause pain just as readily as to have an occasional calming or invigorating effect. Since we expect the artist to be modest so that he may accomplish his unpredictable task, it would be the height of arrogance to claim the right to know and judge for ourselves what will ultimately console and bless us most profoundly.

ON FAITH

A Direction of the Heart

Religion is something infinitely simple, simpleminded. It is not knowledge, not the content of our emotion (for all possible content has been granted already from the beginning wherever a human being engages with life). It is neither duty nor renunciation; it is not limitation, but in the perfect expanse of the universe it is a direction of the heart. How a human being might go and err toward the right and toward the left, and knock himself and fall and get up, and commit injustice here and suffer injustice there, and be abused here and elsewhere wish others ill, and how he might abuse and misunderstand: all this is transferred into the great religions and there maintains and enriches the god that is their center. And man, living still at the farthest periphery of this circle, *belongs* to this powerful center even if he had turned his countenance toward it only once, perhaps while dying. That at specific hours the Arab turns to face the East and prostrates himself, that *is* religion. It is hardly "belief." It has no opposite. It is a natural movement within a human being through which god's wind sweeps three times a day if we are at least this: limber.

Prayer is a ray emanating from our being that has been suddenly set ablaze; it is an infinite and aimless direction; it is a violent parallelism of our aspirations that traverses the universe without arriving anywhere.

Belief!—There is no such thing, I almost said. There is only—love. The way in which our heart is coerced to consider one or another thing to be true, which is usually called belief, does not make sense. First one must find god somewhere and experience him as so infinite, so abundant, so tremendously present, then it may be fear, it may be astonishment, it may be breathlessness, it may in the end be—love, *whatever* one's relation to him then, it hardly matters any longer. But for belief, for this act of being coerced toward god, there is no room wherever someone has embarked on the process of discovering god that then can no longer be stopped regardless of the spot from which one had set out.

.

In everyone's blood there courses a kind of misunderstanding about being "protected" by god, which cheats us of a freedom that belongs to us. The first consequence of this freedom (if we knew how to use it) would be a changed relation to death.

The span of time between birth and death, above which we habitually write "I," is not a measure for god. For him, life + death probably constitutes only the degree of a gap. Maybe there needs to be a continuous *series* of lives and deaths for god to have the impression: *One*—but maybe only the creature in its totality may call itself "I" before him and everything that occurs, appears, and vanishes *within* this creature would be its business . . . We must get used to the fact that we rest between two of god's breaths, in one of the intervals of his breathing, for that means: to be in time. It is conceivable that god is linked to creation only through the act of having externalized it. Then only what has not been created would have a right to consider itself continually linked to god. Presumably, the short span of our existence is precisely the time during which we lose connection with him, fall out of touch with him and into creation *which he leaves alone.* Since we have only memories and premonitions to draw on, the more urgent task might be to apply our senses to what is here and to expand these senses so far that they fuse into a single sense that does nothing but admire.

Just as the expressions of every language are based on social conventions, the word *god* had been agreed upon. It was meant to contain everything that had some kind of effect without anyone being able to name and recognize it otherwise. Consequently, when man was very poor and knew very little, god was very great. With every experience something left his sphere of power. When he finally had been stripped of almost everything, church and state gathered some charitable qualities for him that now nobody may touch.

Do you find it confusing that I say "god" and "gods" and that I concern myself with these statutes (just as with the ghost) for the sake of completeness, all in the assumption that you will be able instantly to form an idea based on these terms? Assume, for a moment, the existence of the supernatural. Let us agree that human beings have from their earliest beginnings created gods that in some instances contained only what is dead and threatening and destructive and terrible, and violence and rage and extrapersonal numbness, all as if knotted into a tight malignant texture. All that is alien, if you wish, but already admitted within this strangeness, as it were, so that one would recognize, endure, and even accept because of its particular, secretive affinity and inclusion this: *one was also this.* But one could not readily figure out what to do with this aspect of one's own experience; these aspects were too large, too dangerous, too multifaceted; they grew beyond one into an excess of meaning.

In addition to the many challenges posed by an existence aimed at use and achievement, it proved impossible always to account for these unwieldy and ungraspable conditions. For this reason, people decided to externalize them occasionally. But because they were excessive, strongest, indeed what is *too* strong, what is powerful, even violent, incomprehensible, frequently tremendous: how should and how could they not, when gathered at one spot, exercise their influence, their effects, their power, their superiority? But now, of course, from the outside. Could one not treat the history of god as that part of the human soul into which no one had ever actually entered but which had always been left to be accessed later, saved up, and ultimately forgone, but for which once there had existed determination and composure? The part of the human disposition, which gradually gave rise to a tension precisely at the spot where it had been displaced to and for which the drive of the individual heart, always dispersing itself anew and suffering petty wounds, is hardly a match.

You see, exactly the same happened with death. Experienced and yet not experienceable for us in its reality, always growing beyond us and still not quite admitted by us, offending and outstripping the meaning of life from its inception, death was similarly exiled and driven out so that it would not continually disrupt us in finding this meaning. Death, which is probably so close to us that we cannot even determine the distance between it and our life's inner center in us, became something external, kept daily at a greater distance, lurking somewhere in the void only to attack one or another according to a malicious principle of selection. Increasingly, there grew the suspicion against death that it was the contradiction of adversaries, the invisible opposite in the air of which our joys perished, that it was the perilous glass of our happiness out of which we could be poured at any moment.

God and death were now outside, had become other, while our life was now the One thing that at the price of this exclusion seemed to become human, intimate, possible, manageable, and in a unified sense ours. But since there remained countless things that needed to be organized and understood in this beginner's course for life, so to speak, in this preschool class for life, and since no strict distinctions could be made between things that were resolved and those that just had been skipped provisionally, even in this limited existence no straight and reliable progress was made; people lived every which way, drawing as much on actual as on erroneously calculated gains. Once a final tally had been reached, there inevitably resurfaced as a fundamental error precisely the condition on which this entire attempt at living had been based. Since god and death seemed to have been subtracted from every meaning that meant anything (not as something in the here and now, but as something later, elsewhere, and other) the small cycle of the present gained ever greater momentum, and so-called progress led to a self-contained world, which forgot that regardless of how it went about it, it had been surpassed by death and god from the beginning. Now this could still have prompted us to come to our senses if we had only succeeded in keeping god and death at a distance as mere ideas—but nature had no knowledge of this repression we had somehow achieved. When a tree blossoms, death blossoms in it as vigorously as life, and the field is full of death that breeds an abundance of life out of its flat countenance, and animals pass patiently from one realm to the other—and everywhere around us death is still at home and eyes us from among the cracks of things, and a rusty nail sticking out of a board somewhere does nothing else, day and night, but to rejoice in it.

And love as well, love, which plants confusion among people by setting up a game of proximity and distances where we matter only inasmuch as if the universe were completely filled up and the only space left were inside of us; love as well is indifferent with regard to the divisions we create and instead tears open for us, shivering and trembling as we are, an unbounded consciousness of the whole. People in love do not live off the limited, curtailed section of the here and now; they draw on their hearts' tremendous store as if no division had ever been instituted. Of them it can be said that god becomes true for them and that death does not hurt them: *for they are full of death by being full of life.*

But this is not a matter of lived experience. It is a secret, though not one that withdraws into itself or wishes to be sequestered. It is a secret that is secure in itself and stands open like a temple whose gates boast of offering entry to us and which sing, between larger-than-life columns, that they are the true portal.

•

Religion is art for those who are not creative. They become productive in prayer: they form their love and their gratitude and their longing and thus gain freedom. They also acquire a kind of short-lived culture by letting go of many goals and instead attaching themselves only to one. But this one goal is not innate to them; everyone has it in common. Yet there exists no common culture. Culture is personality; what we call the culture of many is social consensus without internal justification.

•

Since my visit to Cordoba I am of an almost violent anti-Christianity. I am reading the Koran, which in certain passages assumes a voice within me that I inhabit with as much force as the wind in a pipe organ. Here [in Spain] you think you are in a Christian country, but this is long over. It was Christian as long as one had the courage to commit murder a hundred steps outside of town where the countless modest stone crosses grow. On these crosses is inscribed: here this one or that one died—that was the local brand of Christianity. Now boundless indifference reigns here: empty churches, forgotten churches, starving chapels—really one should no longer take a seat at this table after the meal's been finished and pretend that the finger bowls still lying about would contain nourishment. The fruit has been sucked dry; now it's time, to put it bluntly, to spit out the skins. And yet Protestants and American Christians always create a new brew with this tea that has been steeping for two millennia. Mohammad was certainly the closest alternative, bursting like a river through prehistoric mountains toward the one god with whom one can converse so magnificently every morning without the telephone "Christ" into which people continually call "Hello, who's there?" and there's no answer.

God is the most ancient work of art. He has been preserved very poorly and many parts have been added later, in approximations. But it is of course incumbent upon any educated person to be able to talk about him and to have seen the remnants.

All of love is an effort for me, a challenge, *exhaustion;* only with regard to god are matters a bit easier for me because to love god means to enter, to walk, to stand, to rest, and to be everywhere in god's love.

I am reluctant (to say this at the outset) to consider the love for god a distinct, separate activity of the human heart. I rather suspect that this heart, each time it surprises itself by charting a new, additional circle beyond the already achieved outer circle of its efforts, that with each of its progressions this heart breaks through its object or simply loses it, and then infinitely advances with its love. Whoever wishes to account for the extent to which god profits from love would end up with a startlingly small amount if he failed to take into account these emotional values that basically just pour out as if ownerless. It is not only the case that unmediated attention toward god has decreased in our days, but it has also always been necessary to subtract from this attention those murky and numb parts that the human effort drags into the bed of prayer. One has only to consult any saint's life (for example the blessed Angela of Foligno) to see how tough one has to become not to be seduced by the loveliness of one's own being and not to be torn up by its severity. Such a plain and incessant effort is necessary to connect one's line to god at the point where the heart's springs burst forth, and how very important is it to make this connection so rapidly that one may pour oneself into god fresh and unspent.

For the moment it may be better to refrain from using the word *belief,* deformed as it is within us, in order not to upset right away the innocent proximity to god. By accruing the additional meanings of force and effort, the word *belief* has come to mean very little besides the arduous tasks of a conversion. It has been forgotten that belief is only a slight shading of love on that side where love turns toward the invisible. I understand less and less *what* in fact blocks and distracts us in the love toward god. For a while one could have thought that it was invisibility itself. But don't all of our experiences meanwhile suggest that the presence of a beloved object might prove helpful during the initial stage of love, but that this presence ultimately causes sorrow and harm for the ultimate expansion of our love? Is it not the case that the fates of all lovers, as their accounts have been handed down to us, lend support to these experiences? Can we continue to overlook in the letters of the great abandoned lovers the unconscious rejoicing that resounds in their lamentation every time they realize that their emotions face no longer the beloved, but only their own dizzying, blissful path? Just as in training a horse one might still resort occasionally to offering sugar until this explicit encouragement is no longer needed to trigger a task, we slow learners are still presented with a lovely face for quite a while. But our love's true activity will not begin as long as we still need such an invitation to burst with our entire heart into a love whose direction needs only the barest hint. Or our love would not be the central element it is, if it did not come into existence among the elements of space while hurtling itself outward. If our love were like a spoiled hunger, it would arise only when we are served a meal. But love is the hunger of those who were never sated, a hunger so deep-seated that it no longer calls for bread but instead calls forth the bread.

You should ask yourself this simple question: In a time when you were in love, did you not feel the temptation to transfer into greater circumstances and apply to far greater conditions the sensation that made itself so overwhelmingly felt in relation to a single being? Who has not grown impatient upon seeing his heart's rays refracted right before him and then emptied into another life? Who has not filled this other life with shadows and confusion when he suddenly desired to see his own feeling one more time after it had already passed over and dissolved into that life, and to hold this feeling close to the self at the very spot where it had been torn off? It creates the greatest terror between two individuals that neither one of them can any longer see the love which he had accomplished yesterday. Every new effort breaks away from under one of them and upon this realization he sees only the other where he would find it difficult to see himself. Whoever attempts to love god, however, will not be deprived of any value of his heart. He comes and sees everything that he has accomplished and places high unto the feeling, which had been created yesterday, his subsequent feeling in soundless clarity.

When viewed from a distant future, the Christian attitude, the great Christian event will certainly still be regarded as one of the most wonderful attempts to keep open the path to god. Unfortunately, that it may be the *best* attempt, to prove *this* will be beyond us and our contemporaries since all of Christianity is continuously, before our very eyes, incapable of supplying us with genuine counterweights to the predominant burden of our suffering.

I personally feel a greater affinity to all those religions in which the middleman is less essential or almost entirely suppressed. To have kept him "suffering," if I may put it thus, has increasingly become the effort and achievement of Christian mentality. The arduous path becomes the destination, and certain strengths that ought to be cast into god are delayed and used up along the way.

What presumption to believe that religion would *let* itself be suppressed. Who among us doubts that religion, wherever a spot is bricked up against it, would find a thousand other points of access, that it would besiege us and assail us where we least expect it? Is this not precisely how humans are usually reached by

religion: from attack to attack? Has religion ever occurred differ-
ently in life in the shape of the unexpected, the unspeakable, the
unintended?

•

I will not conceal from you that I consider the stance of the be-
liever to be a danger for the precision of emotion to which we oth-
erwise attribute such significance. When I imagine that I would
become a practicing Catholic today, where is the church that would
not insult me with the stingy pettiness of its depictions and repre-
sentations? It really would need to be a small, ruined chapel of the
kind I found in Spain, the kind which will not be fixed or touched
by any contemporary hand. During the time of Saint Francis this
constituted the ground out of which art produced its most tender
and unencumbered blossoms. To come in contact with the church
today means to become indulgent toward ineptitude; toward the
sweet phrase; toward all the vast expressionlessness of its images,
prayers, and sermons.

•

Please keep in mind that all piousness that does not invent but only
repeats after others and establishes itself in the present via various
forms of hope and exposure is incomprehensible or irrelevant to
me. Insofar as I have insight into it, the relation to god requires
productivity and at least a kind of private genius of invention that
will not be convincing to others. I can imagine this genius to be
stretched to a point where one suddenly does not understand what
is meant by the name of god, and one repeats this name and asks
others to recite it ten times, without any understanding, but in
order to encounter it as entirely new somewhere at its origin, its
source.

.

Who can be sure that we do not always approach the gods from their backs, so to speak, and are thus kept at a distance from their sublime radiant faces by nothing but them and are kept extremely close to the expression that we so desire yet simply stand behind it? What else could this mean but that both our countenance and the divine face look out in the same direction, that they are in agreement; but how should we then step out of that space and toward the god if this is the space he faces before him?

.

In purely spiritual matters the church, when conceived of in its greatest possibility, might reach an immeasurable radius, the greatest on earth, which leads to eternity by way of a nearly imperceptible path—but for someone (such as myself) who is committed to rendering visible what is spiritual, art must make sense as the far greater periphery of life (as the most far-reaching one leading into infinity), for otherwise one would have to deny oneself the pursuit of its laws and manifestations in those works which originated outside of the air of Christian belief and still originate, here and there, in the purest validity. Within the Christian church it is possible to pursue paths toward god of the most blissful ascent and most profound effort: we are given tremendous proof of that in the lives of the saints and in various strong and heartfelt survivals, sometimes even in our most immediate surroundings. But this conviction and experience do not rule out my certainty that the most tremendous relationships with god, if there is strong need and motivation, can take shape also in the extra-Christian soul, in some struggling individual. Just as all of nature, wherever it is simply allowed to have its will, passes inexhaustibly into god.

Never has religion relinquished more of its inner humility and never has it become more presumptuous than when it thinks it can console me. The instant we recognize our inconsolable state would also be the instant when that authentic religious productivity could begin, which by itself does not actually lead to consolation but instead to our honest ability to dispense with all consolation!

Joy is inexpressibly more than happiness. Happiness befalls people, happiness is fate, while people cause joy to bloom inside themselves. Joy is plainly a good season for the heart; joy is the ultimate achievement of which human beings are capable.

Among all of the graces of our "life" there is also the fact that we have been endowed with all of the means to survive the tender abundance of a moment, not only in the realm of memories but also in the continuous interpretation of the pleasures that are bestowed on us.

The reality of an experience of joy is indescribable in the world. Only in joy can creation still take place (while happiness is only the constellation of already existing things that can be promised and interpreted). Joy, however, is a miraculous proliferation of what already exists, a pure addition out of nothingness. Happiness must ultimately have a very weak hold on us since it instantly allows us to reflect on and worry about its duration. Joy is a moment that remains uncommitted; it is timeless from the beginning. It cannot be held but actually cannot be lost either since under its impact our being is, as it were, chemically transformed. In happiness, on the other hand, we taste and enjoy ourselves merely in a new mixture.

Filled with this experience I have kept myself quite safe from disappointment since greater things always retain their right to be *unexpected,* to come and go, and I no longer expect them to emerge as the consequence of preceding greatness. In my experience greatness does not occur as part of a sequence but basically always emerges from an unknowable and immeasurable depth. For that reason I never stop sensing it as a possibility even where it fails to appear.

·

There are times when it constitutes practically a kind of salvation to consider everything a distraction, but those times are exceptions, interludes, convalescences.

ON GOODNESS AND MORALITY

Nothing Good,

Once It Has Come into Existence,

May Be Suppressed

Nothing good, once it has come into existence, may be suppressed. It assumes reality like a tree, on its own: it is, and it flowers, and it bears fruit. Nothing is lost: everything is passed along.

Actually there is no such thing as a good habit: everything good, no matter how often and how unintentionally such a deed is repeated, is new and spontaneous each time.

Nothing makes it more difficult to help than the intention of doing so.

To promote "ideals" means finally nothing else than not letting oneself be distracted in one's inner and internally intended world, even when one is opposed by immensely alien and even hostile realizations that are ultimately in the right.

When the right help is concerned there are no distinctions between something small and something greater, as you allowed me to experience quite wonderfully: *everything attains equal dimensions within it.* The existence of the right piece of string or a sticky label at the moment when one needs it is no less important, calming, and soothing, no less helpful in saving our strength in the most fundamental ways than who knows what kind of enormous assistance such as that given by Berg itself [Rilke's residence from November

1920 to May 1921], for instance, which you found and made possible for me! There are no differences. Most people, even very tender and affectionate people, are exhausted after an act of assistance. Then they must wait for their capacity for help to grow back inside of them. And, there where it truly matters, many things seem to them too trivial to deserve their assistance. They don't know or fail to consider that our internal scales are most confused by the minimal burdens that one has to balance out incessantly with the tiniest weights that slip between our fingers and are too small to be marked by the decimal numbers of their actual weight in fractions of grams. You understood so well, my dear, to be just, how you stood at my scales and *with the same gesture* balanced and removed now a huge burden, now a tiny weight. You returned my scales' pointer to the position above its true center so that I could become distinct to myself with regard to the true weight of my being on the scales' newly calibrated plates.

•

Out of all of these turgid and often overpowering early experiences (for I had to return via hundreds of ways with my sickly body from my education and time), my belief slowly grew that *those* are correct who assume and give voice to this thought during a particular phase of their mind's development: that there is no god and there can never have been one. But this realization is something *infinitely affirmative* for me since it relieves me of all my fears that he could have been used up and passed away, taken from me; now I know *that he will be.* He will be and those who are lonely and extract themselves from time, build him with their heart, head, and hands the way lonely individuals are creative and build artworks (that is: things of the future), build him, *begin him,* the one who will at some point be when time will be filled with eternity.

Among solitary individuals not a single gesture is lost, and the suffering that they bear has effects far into the future. Anything that happens to them is the mirror image of something that takes place in the future. *Everything will be.* And we are the precursors and fortune-tellers.

For this reason all the trust I have in myself is trust in those who are alone; all the love that is in me is love for them. Those who are alone and will not be confused, the prophets who do not announce their revelations, those who are heavy with their silence and sweet with their unspilled longing: they will be the source of redemption.

Ah, how premature Christ was. And how quickly someone so rash encounters even more premature individuals—and then god quickly slips into the past, like everything else about which people talk.

From a diary. Ah, you human beings, when they bring god to you, these obedient well-trained dogs who have fetched him under great danger to themselves, just take him and fling him back out into what is immeasurable, for god *ought* not to be dragged to shore by the obedient, well-trained dogs. He is not in danger on his surging waters, and a great future wave will lift him on to land that is worthy of him.

•

To preserve tradition and what is truly originary (even if not around us, where it is increasingly strangled by current conditions, but *within* us)—and I do not mean what is superficial-conventional—and to continue this tradition intelligently or blindly, depending on one's predisposition, should remain our most decisive task (since after all we are those who will be sacrificed to change).

•

I long for individuals through whom the past in its vast configurations remains attached and related to us, because the future, the more courageously and daringly one imagines it to be, now more than ever depends to such a great degree on whether it will follow the direction of the most profound traditions and cast its movement out of them (rather than out of negation).

An individual partial to matters of the mind would naturally have to oppose and deny revolutions. He, more than anyone else, knows how slowly any change of lasting significance occurs, how such changes are imperceptible and nearly invisible due to their slowness, and how the nature of thinking, in its constructive efforts, hardly permits violence to arise anywhere. And yet on the other hand it is this same thinking individual who grows impatient, owing to his power of insight, when he notices how human affairs tend to go on and persist in misguided and tangled circumstances. Surely we all share the experience that one thing or another, that almost everything has to be changed (indeed at the root). Life, which is infinitely abundant, infinitely generous, may be cruel only on the basis of its inexhaustibility: in how many cases has life lost altogether all claims for its validity because it has been repressed by so many secondary institutions that have grown lethargic in their existence. Is there anyone who would not frequently wish for a ferocious storm that could tear down everything that stands in the way and that is already in decline to clear space for the newly creative, infinitely young, infinitely well-intentioned forces?

But there is nothing more reckless than intentions: you exhaust yourself in them by forming and by reinforcing them, and then there is nothing left for the act of carrying them out.

·

The kinds of experiences that you mention, the conditions of your soul that you let me discern from afar, are properly located outside of the area reached by the activity of "giving answers." This kind of questioning is in fact the questioning nature of our most authentic life—who responds to it? Perhaps happiness or misfortune or an unforeseeable instant of the heart suddenly besieges us with a response, or a response takes shape slowly and imperceptibly within us, or another human being opens it up before us, this response, when it overflows his eyes and transpires on the new page of his heart, which he himself does not know but which we read to him.

·

Violence is a coarse tool and one that cannot be rehearsed. This is why the spirit falls short of it since it does not know acts of violence, for the violence of the spirit is a victory of insurmountable tenderness.

·

Simply having plans already introduces quite a bit of flexibility in us, and who knows how much we transform ourselves within them even if we don't move one bit.

·

If human beings only stopped referring to cruelty in nature as a way of making excuses for their own! The human forgets with what infinite innocence even the most terrifying event in nature takes place. Nature does not look and consider such an event since it has no distance from it—it *is* fully in the most horrible occurrences, that's where its fertility is too, and its generosity; the most horrible occurrence, as it were, [is] ultimately nothing else than an expression of nature's abundance. Its consciousness consists in its completeness; because it contains *everything,* nature contains cruelty as well. Man, however, will never be able to encompass everything and therefore can never be certain when he chooses something dreadful, let's say murder, whether he also contains already the opposite of this abyss. He is thus instantly condemned by his choice because it turns him into an exception, into an isolated, one-dimensional being no longer connected to the whole. A good, purely determined, capable human being would not be capable of excluding evil, disaster, suffering, calamity, death from the conditions of existence. But wherever he would be struck by such a blow or if he were to cause one of them, he would be no different from anyone who stands afflicted in nature. Or he would become someone who afflicts others against his will like the raging stream that breaks its banks with a surge of melting waters that are flooding it unstoppably.

·

The kind of religiosity that cannot be found is perhaps always the kind that is preserved in the best way; when someone is discovered to harbor it, it will be taken away and ripped out of him, and he has to move on and conceive and carry it to term and give birth to his own religion out of himself: but how many have the opportunity to do that?

ON LOVE

There Is No Force in the World

but Love

There is no force in the world but love, and when you carry it within you, if you simply *have* it, even if you remain baffled as to *how* to use it, it will work its radiant effects and help you out of and beyond yourself: one must never lose this belief, one must simply (and if it were nothing else) endure in it!

Is love, taken together with art, not the only license to surpass the human conditions and to be greater, more generous, more unhappy, if necessary, than common man? Let us embrace this possibility heroically—let us renounce none of the advantages afforded to us by our animated state.

To take love seriously, to endure it, and to learn it the way one learns a profession—that is what young people need to do. People have misunderstood the role of love in life like so much else. They have turned love into a game and pleasant distraction because they thought that games and distractions are more blissful than work; but nothing is filled with greater joy and happiness than work, and love, exactly because it is the most extreme joy and happiness, can be nothing but work. A person in love thus has to try to behave as if he had to accomplish a major task: he has to spend a lot of time alone, reflect and think, collect himself and hold on to himself; he has to work; he has to become something!

For love is the actual climate of fate: no matter how far it stretches its path through the heavens along its milky way composed of millions of stars of blood, the land beneath those heavens lies pregnant with disaster. Not even the gods in the metamorphoses of their passion were sufficiently powerful to liberate from the entanglements of this fertile soil the startled, fleeing beloved on our earth.

.

By seizing with our hands, as it were, the once-begun happiness [of love], we might be the first to destroy it; it ought to remain on its creator's anvil, under the blows of his hardworking hammer. Let us place our meager confidence in this admirable craftsman. To be sure, we always feel the poundings of his tool, which he wields mercilessly according to the rules of an accomplished art. But in return we are also from time to time called upon to admire his favorite work as he leads it toward its ultimate perfection: how much we had already admired it the first time! We are hardly even collaborators in our love and it is for this very reason that our love remains above trivial dangers. Let us try to get to know its laws, its seasons, its rhythm, and the march of its constellations across its vast, starry sky. I know well that in speaking to you in this fashion, there remains an absolutely unequal task for the two of us: you are too much woman not to suffer infinitely through that deferral of love that this task seems to entail. And by gathering around my work, I myself secure the means of my more definitive happiness, while you, at least at this moment, in turning toward your life find yourself encumbered by half-frozen tasks. Don't let this discourage you; it will surely change. Through the transfiguration of your heart you will gradually influence the obstinate givens of reality;

everything that seems impenetrable to you will be rendered transparent by your blazing heart . . . Don't think too much about the moment and refrain from judging life during those hazy hours that afford us no glimpse of its vastness.

·

When a person takes leave of himself he is nothing any longer; when two people give themselves up in order to be joined as one there is no more ground beneath them and their togetherness is an incessant falling.

·

It is always again the question of the "whole" with which we are concerned, but this whole, even if we sometimes grasp it completely inside in a burst of happiness or a purer effort of the will, is in reality interrupted by all the errors, mistakes, shortcomings, and maliciousness between people, by all that is helpless and murky—yes, by nearly all of our daily concerns.

It is a disturbing thought that the instant of love that we experience so fully, profoundly, and peculiarly as our own could be so entirely determined beyond the individual person by the future (the future child) and on the other side by the past. But even *then:* this moment of love would retain its indescribable profundity as an escape into the self. Which I strongly tend to believe. This would correspond to our experience of how the incommensurate moments of our most profound rapture occur as if they had been lifted out of time itself. Such experiences truly run perpendicular to the directions of life, just as death runs perpendicular in relation to them. Such experiences have more in common with death than with any aim or objective of our vitality. Only death (as long as it is recognized not as a state of being withered but presumed to be the intensity that quite exceeds us) affords us a perspective to do justice to love. But here again our vision is obstructed by the common understanding of these quantities. Our traditions have grown weak in their power to transmit; they are brittle twigs no longer nourished from the roots. And when to all of this is added the absentmindedness, distractedness, and impatience of man, and the fact that woman is profoundly giving only in the rare relationships of happiness, and that next to these thus split and shaken individuals the child stands as something that already surpasses them while it remains just as helpless—well, then one might humbly admit that things are quite difficult for us.

Through physiological research we make ever more astonishing discoveries with regard to the distribution of masculine and feminine elements within all beings; we are so far from knowing whether there is an unequivocal here and there. In this domain everything is calibrated with utmost precision and in great secrecy, and it can very easily happen, and not only "abnormally," that the kind of complementary affinity occurs between two young women that justifies even the most intimate sensuality. I suspect that such raptures are filled with much more innocence than many "normal" relations and that once it becomes possible to acknowledge how entirely natural and guileless such delights are, it might also be possible to strangely unburden the confused, overwrought efforts at love between woman and man. For this love surely faces as its most insurmountable and disastrous difficulty the tremendous emphasis of its one "goal," as if all the paths and dead ends of our emotions would have to succeed in reaching this sweet region. But in this way love is transformed from being something secret into something conspicuous, and in this way alone love has been immensely distorted. Since people in love actually do not see an end to what they give and what they may receive, and since in their hands everything becomes nameless, they actually could not know *even when facing each other* (this is how I always imagine it) whether among the countless instances of bliss experienced in their union there might also have been one which (rightly or wrongly, perhaps both) is considered the most extreme.

Now you may already have surmised a little of *what* I expect of this genuine intercourse of love within one gender: that it prepares within the individuals who undergo it (maybe only quite temporarily) a different kind of valuation where the one goal—which can never fully be reached there—does not entirely predominate, although it could be *there,* according to its potency. Instead, within this always more intimate exchange many things would emerge and get used up (especially when the man is concerned) that otherwise plainly overwhelm and flood the other gender without strictly having intended to do so. I should like to think of such periods of love as a veritable school for love that covers the most sensuous touches and embraces as well as the spirit's tenderly shared hovering, and where the little temple is placed alternately among youthful male lovers and then among females, as if their more fraught attractions later in life depended a tiny bit upon the tender experiences and exercises that occur easily and pre-seriously among themselves.

In this area everything is in such disarray for us that one should not hesitate to make even the most daring suggestion, as long as it might pave a way toward change in this legally protected rubble. And ultimately what is our measure for determining whether something is "daring"—it is morality, which has long been known to create great confusion when it intervenes in the realm of love and distorts the significance of appearances that cannot be compared when taken out of context. If we ever have a sense of being blocked by morality, we finally ought to become suspicious only about the blockage but not about our impulses. The sense of a totality, the always renewed feeling of the unity of our own life and those indescribable moments during which death no longer prompts our suspicion: these are the building blocks for everybody's private court of law where his responsibility will be judged.

·

There is no more wretched prison than the fear of hurting someone who loves you.

·

For all transformations that take place between two individuals this remains true: One must *never* view and assess a relationship in all of its details from the *outside:* what two people could give and grant each other in their mutually trusting confidence remains for all time a secret of their always indescribable intimacy. If they thought at a particular moment that they could give each other pleasure even more tenderly, this might have been a small error since they did not serve their happiness in this way but their desire and thus cast disturbances into their blood that could prove distressing after the fact—but who is to judge that? Perhaps they were justified after all in thus surrendering, which is so indescribably innocent, like everything in love that is born of a simple having-to-do and not-knowing-any-differently—nobody may dare to judge from the outside what happened there. Such rapture and such joy, no matter how far they go, may yield a moment of transformation that concerns nothing but *the soul.* And since this had seemed like a new kind of experience reached through what is called sensuality one may have been all along in a truly advanced state ahead of one's soul, which had been transported there through rapture. All of this is so much more secretly connected that we must face these forces with humility. Our resistance will be provided by innocence itself, which is indestructible within us as long as we do not allow others to convince us of our guilt. The uncertainties and insecurities in these areas have increased so terribly in our time that a young person can almost never count on having the kind of adviser and protector whom he would need, not even in the figure of his mother (who is helpless like the whole world). For this reason alone, one ought to rely unerringly and guilelessly on one's innocence to get one's bearings. Sensible people have long struggled to relieve love relations within one gender of the ugly suspicions placed there by convention—but even this effort and viewpoint does not seem the right one. It isolates a process that ought to be considered always only within the full range of its contexts, and it turns an inexpressibly unique occurrence into something general and even ordinary only because it could engulf anyone. And ultimately this approach retains only the physical manifestation of such an event and forgets in what inaccessible and exuberant relations this one thing (which only appears capable of being described) is placed. We do not know *where* to locate the center of a love relation and what would constitute its most extreme, unsurpassable, and most ecstatic dimension: sometimes this center may be found in the final and sweetest physical intimacy (also between women) but *nothing* ought to be the judge of that with the exception of the discreet responsibility of these lovers in their pleasure. This mutual surrender would not mean that they have gone astray; at most, they could be deterred from their path by the insecurity whether they in fact afforded each other this lasting intensification that is the ultimate desire and longing of love. But only if this mutual giving would cause them to become more inaccessible, murky, and opaque to each other would they be wrong in daring to cross over into such abandonment: *Then,* however, there would be the danger that they remain stuck in it. For *no* tenderness of love ought to have power over love itself, and no tenderness must impose itself with the force of mindless repetition, but an entirely new tenderness must be born always anew out of the inexhaustibility of one's emotions.

•

Two individuals who are quiet to the same degree have no need to talk about the melody that defines their hours. This melody is what they have in common in and of itself. Like a burning altar it exists between them, and they nourish the sacred flame respectfully with their occasional syllables.

•

Is it not wonderful to assure oneself that love can lead to such strength, and that at bottom it concerns something that exceeds us entirely, and that nonetheless the heart is bold enough to embark on this going-beyond-us, this tempest for which an entire genesis would be required?

•

It is truly dreadful that we do not have a religion where these experiences, as literal and tangible as they are (at the same time so ineffable and so inviolable), may be lifted up and into god, into the protection of a phallic deity, which might have to be the *first* with which a whole group of gods will intrude again upon mankind, after such a long delay. What else could be of assistance when religion fails to help us by obscuring these experiences instead of transfiguring them and depriving us of them instead of implanting them in us more magnificently than we might dare imagine. In this respect, we are indescribably abandoned and have been betrayed: hence our disaster. When the religions died away and finally became systems of moral philosophy while more and more of their surfaces burned out, they displaced this experience, which is the innermost of their and our own existence, to the cold basis of morality and thus necessarily shifted it to the periphery. One will gradually realize that the great catastrophe of our time occurs *here* and not in the social or economic domain—in this banishing of the act of love to the periphery. All the strength of insightful individuals is now wasted by shifting the act of love back at least into their *own* center (since it's already been shifted away from the general center of the world, from where the world would instantly be set coursing with gods!). Those who move through life blindly, on the contrary, somehow enjoy the accessibility of "pleasure" that is now located on the periphery and takes revenge (unwittingly clear-minded) for their worthlessness in that area by at once seeking out and yet despising this pleasure. Superficial renunciation does *not* constitute progress, and it makes no sense to summon one's "willpower" to this end (which is in any case much too young and recent a force in comparison with the ancient righteousness of our drives). Renunciation of love and fulfillment of love: they are *both* wonderful and without equal only where the entire experience of love may assume a central position along with *all* of its nearly indistinguishable thrills (which alternate in such a way that precisely *there* the psychic and the physical can no longer be distinguished): that is then also the place (in the ecstasy of a few lovers and saints of *all* times and *all* religions) where renunciation and fulfillment become identical. Where infinity occurs *entirely* (whether as a negative or positive), the prefix drops away, that which had been the, ah, all too humanly achieved way, which now has been followed—and what remains is the state of having arrived, *being itself*!

.

If I offered no resistance to the beloved, this happened because among all of the ways in which one human being can take possession of another, her unstoppable approach alone seemed to me to be in the right. In my exposed state, I also did not want to *avoid* her; but I longed to penetrate and pass through her! So that she would open a window for me into the expanded universe of existence . . . (not a mirror).

.

What a pathetic figure man cuts in the history of love. He has almost no strength but the superiority that tradition ascribes to him, and even this superiority he bears so carelessly that it would be outrageous if this distractedness and absent-heartedness were not sometimes partly justified by important events. Yet nobody will talk me out of what is plain to see between this most intense lover [the Portuguese nun Marianna Alcoforado] and her shameful partner: that this relation definitively proves how on the part of women, there is everything that has been achieved, endured, and accomplished in love, while on the part of men, there is only an absolute incapacity to love. She is awarded the diploma in the art of love, to use a banal analogy, while he carries an elementary grammar book of love in his pocket from which he has at best picked up a few words to construct an occasional sentence, as pretty and thrilling as those well-known sentences on the first pages of a language primer.

.

To be loved means to be ablaze. To love is: to cast light with inexhaustible oil. To be loved is to pass away; to love is to last.

⋅

This is the miracle that happens each time in the case of people who are truly in love: the more they give, the more they own of this delicious nourishing love from which flowers and children receive their strength and which could help everyone if people would accept it without doubt.

⋅

It is part of the nature of every definitive love that sooner or later it can reach the beloved only in infinity.

⋅

Woman has undergone, achieved, and seen through to its end what is most proper to her. Man, who could always bring up the excuse of being occupied with more important matters and (let's be frank) who also was never adequately prepared for love, has since antiquity not permitted himself (with the exception of the saints) to enter into love. The troubadours knew exactly how little they were permitted to advance, and Dante [Alighieri], for whom this became an extremely pressing need, could only get around to love on the awesome curve of his gigantically evasive poem. Everything else is derivative and secondary in this sense.

⋅

It has been my experience over and over again that there is hardly anything more difficult than to love someone. It is work, day labor, truly a daily chore: god knows, there is no other word for it. Young people are not being prepared for the great difficulty of love. Our conventions have tried to turn this complicated and extreme relation into something easy and effortless and created the illusion that anyone is capable of love. But this is not the case. To love is difficult, and it is more difficult than other tasks because in other conflicts nature herself urges us to pull ourselves together and gather ourselves with all our strength. But once love becomes more intense we are increasingly tempted to surrender ourselves entirely. But really, can this amount to anything beautiful: to give oneself to the other not as a whole and coherent self but by chance, piece by piece, just as it happens to come about? Can such a giving away of one's self, which so closely resembles a throwing away and tearing apart, amount to anything good, can it be happiness, joy, progress? No, it cannot . . . When you give someone flowers, you arrange them beforehand, don't you? But young people in love throw themselves at one another with the impatience and haste of their passion, and they do not even notice what lack of mutual consideration characterizes this disorderly surrender. They notice it only with amazement and displeasure when they perceive the tension that arises between them owing to all of this disorder. And once discord exists between them, the situation grows more confusing with each passing day; neither of them is able to hold on to anything that is not shattered but pure and unspoiled. And amid all of the hopelessness of things breaking up, they try to maintain the illusion of their happiness (for all of this was supposed to be in the name of happiness). They hardly manage to recall what they had meant by happiness. Each of them grows increasingly unjust toward the other in his or her uncertainty. While they mean to please each other, they touch each other only impatiently and in a dominating manner. And in the effort to escape from the intolerable and unbearable condition of their confusion, they commit the greatest mistake that can be made within a relationship: they become impatient. They push themselves to reach closure by arriving at a binding decision (as they believe); they try to define once and for all their relationship whose unexpected changes made them scared so that from now on it can remain the same "for*ever*" (as they say). This is only the final error in this long chain of interlocking mistakes. Even what is dead cannot be held on to conclusively (for it disintegrates and changes in its nature); how much less may something living and alive be treated definitively once and for all. Life means transformation, and human relations that are an extract of life are the most changeable things of all; they rise and fall from minute to minute, and for people in love there are no two moments that resemble one another within their relationship's intimacy. Nothing habitual and nothing that had already occurred before ever takes place between such individuals but only countless new, unexpected, unheard-of things. There exist relationships that must amount to a very great and almost unbearable happiness, but they can take place only between people blessed with abundance and between individuals each one of whom is rich, focused, and mindful; they can be united only by two expansive, deep, and individual worlds. Young people—this is obvious—cannot attain such a relationship. Yet if they understand their life correctly they can gradually grow into such happiness and prepare themselves for it. When they are in love they must not forget that they are beginners, bunglers of life, apprentices in love—they must *learn* love, and that requires (as for *all* learning) quiet, patience, and concentration!

●

Once in love, once ablaze, one must no longer consider oneself unhappy. Whoever had gained entry once into the joyousness of love *is in it* and for such an individual all deprivation and all longing constitute henceforth only the weight and gravity of his fullness! It's possible that love will then turn into pain for him, into suffering and despair, and that he can no longer apply this fullness *at the point* where it had been originally desired and expected. But isn't every young man always in the position of a "sorcerer's apprentice" when his urgent heart unleashes tempests that he cannot master? He saves himself from them (maybe *has to* save himself) to adhere to that other standard in his life, that logical, apparently sober principle of being productive, which contradicts love and at times tolerates the senses only as a way of balancing the exaggerated tensions arising on the other side.

•

What ruthless magnificence and yet how *terrible* to ignite love: what conflagration, what disaster, what doom. To be on fire *yourself*, of course, if one is capable of it: that may well be worth life and death.

•

The more one is, the more abundant is everything one experiences. If you want to have a deep love in your life, you must save up for it and collect and gather honey.

•

It is a characteristic of every deepened love that it makes us just and clairvoyant.

•

People in love live badly and in danger. Ah, if they could just go beyond themselves and become lovers. There is nothing but security around those who love.

•

People are so terribly far apart from each other, and people in love are often at the furthest distance. They throw all that is their own to the other person and fail to catch it, and it ends up in a pile somewhere between them and finally keeps them from seeing and approaching each other.

.

It is possible to love to *such* an extent that the shortcomings of one's beloved begin to appear touching, even wonderful, and become an incentive to be all the more loving!

.

I have never understood how a genuine, elementary, thoroughly true love can remain unrequited since such a love is nothing but the urgent and blessed appeal for another person to be beautiful, abundant, great, intense, unforgettable: nothing but the surging commitment for him to amount to something. And tell me, who would be in a position to refuse this appeal when it is directed at him, when it elects him from among millions where he might have lived obscured by his fate or unattainable in the midst of fame . . . No one can seize, take, and contain within himself such love: it is so absolutely intended to be passed onward beyond the individual and needs the beloved only for the ultimate charge that will propel its future orbiting among the stars.

SOURCES

Where no addressee is listed, the excerpt is taken from Rilke's diaries or other prose texts.

Do not: August 12, 1904, Franz Xaver Kappus   3
[T]here are: December 16, 1920, Baladine
    Klossowska   3

ON LIFE AND LIVING: *You Have to Live Life to the Limit*

There is only: 1914   7
If we wish: 1898   7
Wishes! Desires!: December 19, 1919, Nanny Wunderly-Volkart   8
Life takes pride: June 26, 1907, Clara Rilke   8
A conscious fate: May 26, 1922, Lotti von Wedel   8
Seeing is: March 9, 1899, Elena Woronina   8
To look at something: March 8, 1907, Clara Rilke   9
It does not happen: October 23, 1900, Otto Modersohn   9
Each experience: January 18, 1902, Carl Mönckeberg   10
Wishes are: March 9, 1899, Elena Woronina   10
Be out of sync: 1902   10
After all: January 2, 1912, Julie Freifrau von Nordeck   10
My god: January 2, 1922, Nanny Wunderly-Volkart   10
Life has been: December 9, 1920, Cäsar von Sedlakowitz   10
How numerous: August 20, 1906, Mathilde Vollmoeller   10
The longer I live: December 21, 1913, Ilse Erdmann   11
It is not possible: August 25, 1915, Annette de Vries   11
I have: November 25, 1920, Marie Therese Mirbach-Geldern   12

Is not everything: February 17, 1921, Baladine Klossowska   12
What else does it mean: February 11, 1924, Lisa Heise   12
We lead our lives: September 13, 1907, Clara Rilke   12
It is possible: January 14, 1920, Nanny Wunderly-Volkart   13
Finally: June 28, 1922, Nanny Wunderly-Volkart   13
How tremendous: December 29, 1913, Marie von Thurn
          und Taxis   13
You have to live life: 1904   13
Life has long since: May 19, 1922, Lisa Heise   14
The following realization: 1898   14
I want to thank you: Feb 22, 1907, Clara Rilke   14
Life is so very true: March 19, 1922, Tora Holmström   15
Life goes on: July 25, 1903, Lou Andreas-Salomé   15
Do not believe: May 21, 1921, R. R. Junghanns   16
Wherever: March 17, 1907, Paula Modersohn-Becker   17
How peculiar: January 5, 1921, Inga Junghanns   17
Ah, we count the years: October 19, 1907, Clara Rilke   17
We make our way: February 8, 1906, Karl von der Heydt   18
Even the past is still a being: 1919   18
It is, after all: June 22, 1917, Sophie Liebknecht   18
How is it possible: November 8, 1915, Lotte Hepner   18
It is possible: February 25, 1907, Clara Rilke   19
I believe: August 11, 1907, Stefan Zweig   20
Something is: August 8, 1909, Julie von Nordeck zur Rabenau   20
It seems to me: August 24, 1904, Tora Holmström   21
Even on days: July 17, 1922, Ruth Sieber-Rilke   21
And yet life: December 8, 1911, Sidonie Nádherny von Borutin   21
We of the here and now: November 13, 1925, Witold Hulewicz   22
How good life is: 1908   23
All of our insights: 1906   23
I basically: April 11, 1910, Manon zu Solms-Laubach   23
History is: June 26, 1915, Marianne Mitford   23

In life: April 1, 1924, Nanny Wunderly-Volkart 24
How old: March 25, 1910, Anton Kippenberg 25
What we all need: January 14, 1919, Adelheid von Marwitz 25
I believe in old age: 1905 25
How wonderful: September 25, 1905, Gudrun von Uexküll 25
Is it not peculiar: December 2, 1895, Julius Bauschinger 26
We have to be: April 1910, Sidonie Nádherny von Borutin 26
I confess: October 9, 1918, Aline Dietrichstein 27

ON BEING WITH OTHERS:
To Be a Part, That Is Fulfillment for Us

To be a part: 1911 31
All disagreement: 1898 31
Injustice has: January 27, 1926, Aurelia Gallarati-Scotti 31
This is one: January 30, 1923, Nanny Wunderly-Volkart 31
If one could: December 16, 1923, Margot Sizzo 31
But there: November 4, 1909, Elisabeth Schenk zu Schweinsberg 32
Before a human: February 14, 1926, Aurelia Gallarati-Scotti 32
And yet: 1918 33
As soon: December 26, 1921, R. R. Junghanns 33
When it is: January 21, 1922, R. R. Junghanns 33
If you find: September 13, 1922, E. M. 34
Nothing locks: September 13, 1922, E. M. 35
Marriage is difficult: February 4, 1904, Ellen Key 35
I am of the opinion: August 17, 1901, Emanuel von Bodman 35
There is no: August 25, 1915, Annette de Vries-Hummes 37
Ultimately: June 25, 1902, Otto Modersohn 37
When two or three people: 1898 37
We are so rarely: August 20, 1915, Annette de Vries-Hummes 38
To be able to help: August 20, 1915, Annette de Vries-Hummes 38
In a world: October 21, 1924, Hermann Pongs 38
No book: December 28, 1921, Ilse Blumenthal-Weiss 38

Our emotions: August 23, 1915, Annette de Vries-Hummes 39
Perhaps the poet: 1911 39
To be close: August 25, 1915, Annette de Vries-Hummes 39
There is a single: May 11, 1910, Mimi Romanelli 40
From one human being: July 25, 1903, Lou Andreas-Salomé 40
It seems to me: October 21, 1924, Hermann Pongs 40
Ultimately: April 29, 1904, Friedrich Westhoff 41
The privilege: December 9, 1925, Berta Flamm 41
Departures create: October 18, 1900, Clara Westhoff 41
How telling: 1902 42
The more human we become: 1902 42
We have all known: March 7, 1919, Inga Junghanns 42

ON WORK: *Get Up Cheerfully on Days You Have to Work*

Perhaps creating something: 1902 45
Ah, this longing: 1902 45
This is the one: February 21, 1907, Karl von der Heydt 45
We have to mix: December 19, 1906, Clara Rilke 45
Before they had: March 11, 1907, Clara Rilke 45
Get up cheerfully: 1898 46
What one writes: October 21, 1907, Reinhold von Walter 46
In the boundless heavens: September 4, 1908, Clara Rilke 47
It often happens: April 14, 1910, Marietta von Nordeck 47
I have often wondered: August 24, 1904, Tora Holmström 48
To come: December 18, 1907, Sidonie Nádherny von Borutin 48
The widely asked: March 22–24, 1920, Anita Forrer 49
When I entered: December 19, 1925, Georg Reinhart 51
If someone: March 17, 1922, Margot Sizzo 51
Art is directed: August 30, 1910, Marie von Thurn und Taxis 52
Places, landscapes: June 13, 1908, Sidonie Nádherny von Borutin 53
Fame is nothing: 1902 53
Fame today: November 12, 1925, Margot Sizzo 53

You know: December 22, 1908, Sidonie Nádherny von Borutin   54
No one can lift: May 17, 1898   54

On Difficulty and Adversity:
The Measure by Which We May Know Our Strength

A failure: January 2, 1909, Lili Kanitz-Menar   57
Apparently the power: September 10, 1921, Lou Andreas-Salomé   57
To feel: October 27, 1924, Nanny Wunderly-Volkart   57
The experience: March 16, 1907, Karl von der Heydt   57
But of course: May 16, 1920; Nanny Wunderly-Volkart   57
I realize: June 28, 1922, Nanny Wunderly-Volkart   58
This is not to say: December 27, 1920, Francine Brüstlein   58
All of misery: June 28, 1915, Thankmar von Münchhausen   58
In life: January 19, 1920, Anita Forrer   59
This "taking life: March 13, 1920, Rudolf Bodländer   59
Somewhere in space: October 21, 1914, Helene Nostiz   59
One must never despair: April 29, 1904, Friedrich Westhoff   59
The most: September 6, 1915, Marie von Thurn und Taxis   60
It is dispiriting: June 6, 1921, Nanny Wunderly-Volkart   60
Are there circumstances: December 5, 1914, Marianne von
    Goldschmidt-Rothschild   60
How every creature: 1921   60
The suffering: November 6, 1914, Karl and Elisabeth von der
    Heydt   61
The most wonderful: February 14, 1920, Anita Forrer   61
What a horrible: December 12, 1921, Nanny Wunderly-Volkart   61
And yet: December 9, 1913, Sidonie Nádherny von Borutin   62
"Who would: late November 1920, Magdalene Schwamm-
    berger   62
And while: February 19, 1922; Margot Sizzo   62
The strings of sorrow: November 17, 1912, N.N.   63
Whatever is heavy: August 21, 1919, Yvonne von Wattenwyl   63

It is confusing: August 21–22, 1919, Yvonne von Wattenwyl 63

Among lonely people: September 11, 1915, Ilse Erdmann 64

ON CHILDHOOD AND EDUCATION:
This Joy in Daily Discovery

Childhood: February 11, 1914, Magda von Hattingberg 67

Most people: November 12, 1901, Helmut Westhoff 67

Art is childhood: February 14, 1904, Ellen Key 67

There is: 428; May 20, 1921, Nanny Wunderly-Volkart 68

Why, by god: February 20, 1921, Baladine Klossowska 68

We do not claim life: August 20, 1915, Annette de Vries-
  Hummes 68

I maintain: December 2, 1921, Marie Therese Mirbach-
  Geldern 68

To have a childhood: December 16, 1902, Friedrich Huch 69

Childhood is a land: 1898 69

This is finally true: 1898 69

Parents should never: 1898 70

In light of the current state of affairs: 1902 70

Ah, if our parents: 1898 70

Each person ought to be guided: 1902 70

How many children: December 23, 1920, Regina Ullmann 71

Every historical period: 1902 71

As peculiar: May–June 1905 72

All knowledge: May–June 1905 72

Don't children: February 9, 1914, Magda von Hattingberg 73

I would like to believe: October 9, 1915, Ilse Erdmann 73

Children are at rest: February 8, 1914, Magda von Hattingberg 73

This is what it means: November 1, 1916, Aline Dietrichsen 73

Just think: November 20, 1904, to a young girl 73

With only: January 17, 1900, Sidonie Nádherny von Borutin 74

There is no: August 20, 1909, Sidonie Nádherny von Borutin 74

ON NATURE: *It Knows Nothing of Us*

It is difficult: August 29, 1900, Sofia Nikolaevna 77
We play with dark forces: 1902 77
The final: June 3, 1906, Sidonie Nádherny von Borutin 78
What we experience as spring: 1900 78

ON SOLITUDE: *The Loneliest People Above All Contribute Most to Commonality*

As a child: April 3, 1903, Ellen Key 83
Whether you are surrounded: 1898 84
The loneliest people: 1898 84
I have little to add: October 21, 1907, Reinhold von Walter 84
I consider: February 12, 1902, Paula Modersohn-Becker 85
In such a case: August 17, 1901, Emanuel von Bodman 85
One may be much more literal: March 7, 1921, Lisa Heise 85
Incidentally: March 20, 1922, Elizabeth de Waal 86
Everyone should find: April 8, 1903, Clara Rilke 86
Solitude is: March 17, 1907, Paula Modersohn-Becker 87
It happens: March 7, 1921, Lisa Heise 87
It is more: December 2, 1921, Marie Therese Mirbach-Geldern 88
Poet or painter: 1902 88
To be alone: December 30, 1911, Marie von Thurn und Taxis 89
Art is not: January 1914 89
How stubbornly: September 24, 1908, Rosa Schobloch 89
The art object: August 2, 1919, Lisa Heise 89
Why do people in love break up: November 4, 1909, Elisabeth Schenk zu Schweinsberg 91

ON ILLNESS AND RECOVERY: *Pain Tolerates No Interpretation*

Even a drawn-out: July 5, 1917, Anton Kippenberg 95
It is insufferable: April 11, 1912, Elsa Bruckmann 95
How dangerous: May 11, 1926, Nanny Wunderly-Volkart 95

I used to wonder: March 1, 1912, Lou Andreas-Salomé 95
I am not afraid: February 19, 1914, Magda von Hattingberg 96
It is true: January 4, 1923, Marguerite Masson-Ruffy 96
There is nothing: January 28, 1922, Lotti von Wedel 97
[There is] that: January 15, 1922, Nanny Wunderly-Volkart 97
Illness is the means: 1907 98
Not to award: 1919 98
For me: May 9, 1926, Margot Sizzo 99
No matter: March 12, 1922, Aurelia Gallarati-Scotti 100
In dying: October 9, 1915, Ilse Erdmann 100
To take seriously: March 20, 1919, Ilse Erdmann 101
Finally: April 12, 1922, Nanny Wunderly-Volkart 102
To endure: August 5, 1909, Karl von der Heydt 102
Even—: January 28, 1912, Hedda Sauer 103

ON LOSS, DYING, AND DEATH: *Even Time Does Not "Console" . . . It Puts Things in Their Place and Creates Order*

It has: September 23, 1908, Elisabeth Schenk zu Schweinsberg 107
We simply: December 27, 1913, Thankmar von Münchhausen 107
I once stood: February 14, 1920, Anita Forrer 108
Words: January 6, 1923, Margot Sizzo 108
What, finally: 1921 112
One never knows: March 26, 1920, Nanny Wunderly-Volkart 112
There is: December 23, 1923, Magdalena Schwammberger 112
My dear S: August 1, 1913, Sidonie Nádherny von Borutin 113
Alas, only those: July 16, 1908, Lili Kanitz-Menar 114
Now my attitude: July 16, 1908, Lili Kanitz-Menar 114
Through loss: June 16, 1922, Alexandrine Schwerin 115
See, I think: October 22, 1923, Claire Goll 115
Does our human state: July 7, 1924, Catherine Pozzi 116
It is the peculiar prerogative: May 1, 1921, Erwin von Aretin 116

Yes: April 14, 1924, Rudolf Burckhardt 117

There is no task: June 4, 1921, Reinhold von Walter 117

It is said either: June 2, 1921, Nanny Wunderly-Volkart 117

I have repeatedly read: April 12, 1923; Margot Sizzo 118

To understand: October 9, 1915, Ilse Erdmann 120

How very much I hope: February 3, 1912, André Gide 120

We are: May 1, 1924, Dory von der Mühll 120

In life there is death: December 8, 1907, Mimi Romanelli 121

To understand: January 21, 1919, Lou Andreas-Salomé 121

Death is: November 13, 1925, Witold Hulewicz 121

Never has: September 11, 1919, Adelheid von der Marwitz 122

The most profound: August 21, 1924, Catherine Pozzi 122

ON LANGUAGE: *That Vast, Humming, and Swinging Syntax*

To be someone: 1902 127

In what soil: December 16, 1913, Marie von Thurn und Taxis 127

There can be no: November 7, 1925, Nanny Wunderly-Volkart 127

When writing poetry: December 29, 1908, Auguste Rodin 128

What one writes: December 26, 1911, anonymous 128

Increasingly: September 25, 1921, Nora Purtscher-Wydenbruck 128

There is so much: September 8, 1903, Lou Andreas-Salomé 129

I suppose: January 17, 1926, Aurelia Gallarati-Scotti 130

It is frightening: December 7, 1907, Mimi Romanelli 130

It is contrary: August 5, 1904, Clara Rilke 130

Do not say: March 23, 1921, Rolf von Ungern-Sternberg 130

To be honest: November 30, 1913, Ilse Erdmann 131

At bottom: May 27, 1899, Frieda von Bülow 132

This, indeed: September 1916, Elisabeth Jacobi 132

ON ART: *Art Presents Itself as a Way of Life*

The creations of art: June 24, 1907, Clara Rilke 135

The work of art: 1902 135

Art presents itself: 1898   135

Asceticism: 1921   135

Art is childhood: 1898   136

The life: February 20, 1921, Baladine Klossowska   136

What I write: March 13, 1922, Rudolf Bodländer   137

We most certainly need: June 24, 1907, Clara Rilke   137

As much: November 11, 1921, Gertrud Ouckama Knoop   138

So much has been written: May 6, 1899, Elena Woronina   138

It is always forgotten: July 28, 1901, Alexander Benois   139

The fact is: July 28, 1901, Alexander Benois   140

I consider art to be: 1898   140

An art object: January 27, 1909, Anton Kippenberg   140

One is tempted to explain the work of art: 1898   140

Don't wait: November 18, 1920, Baladine Klossowska   141

As an artist: 1921   141

I have often: November 18, 1920, Baladine Klossowska   142

Even when music: February 13, 1914, Magda von Hattingberg   143

In art: August 21, 1924, Catherine Pozzi   143

Who among us: February 14, 1924, Werner Milch   144

[I]f there is no art: January 12, 1900, Alfred Lichtwark   144

An individual: August 20, 1915, Annette de Vries-Hummes   144

Just as: August 20, 1915, Annette de Vries-Hummes   145

For most people: 1921   145

I cannot: March 1921, Marie Therese Mirbach-Geldern   146

Freedom should: April 29, 1921, Rolf von Ungern-Sternberg   146

The question: November 1, 1916, Aline Dietrichsen   146

Artistic work: January 1, 1912, Manon zu Solms-Laubach   147

I have noticed: October 21, 1907, Reinhold von Walter   148

The practice of artistic seeing: October 19, 1907, Clara Rilke   148

The "only work": March 13, 1922, Rudolf Bodländer   149

Quite early on: January 17, 1923, Dr. Faust   150

The deeply moving: January 12, 1922, Robert Heinz Heygrodt   150

It seems to me: January 12, 1922, Robert Heinz Heygrodt 151
It is possible: June 28, 1907, Clara Rilke 151
As soon: December 24, 1921, Robert Heinz Heygrodt 152
It seems: June 6, 1906, Clara Rilke 152
What is so terrible: December 28, 1911, Lou Andreas-Salomé 153
Art is not: August 19, 1909, Jakob Uexkuell 154
A thing is definite: August 8, 1903, Lou Andreas-Salomé 154
Look: I also: August 11, 1903, Lou Andreas-Salomé 154
This *is the basis:* November 22, 1920, R.S. 155
All creative activities: March 31, 1921, Erwein von Aretin 156
The way: July 26, 1923, Hans Reinhart 156
Our time: 1909 157
For an object to become art: März 23, 1922, Rudolf Bodländer 157
The things: November 13, 1925, Witold Hulewicz 158
Art always promises: November 5, 1918, Anni Mewes 158
Revolution: January 5, 1919, Emil Lettré 158
A sense of security: October 9, 1916, Ilse Erdmann 158
There truly: November 20, 1905, Karl von der Heydt 159
The confusion: July 26, 1923, Hans Reinhart 160

On Faith: *A Direction of the Heart*

Religion is: December 28, 1921, Ilse Blumenthal-Weiss 163
Prayer is a ray: January 5, 1910, Mimi Romanelli 163
Belief!: December 28, 1921, Ilse Blumenthal-Weiss 163
In everyone's blood: June 2, 1921, Nanny Wunderly-Volkart 164
Just as the expressions: 1921 165
Do you find it: November 8, 1915, Lotte Hepner 165
Religion is art: 1921 168
Since my: December 17, 1921, Marie von Thurn und Taxis 168
God is the most ancient work of art: 1921 169
All of love: March 21, 1913; Marie von Thurn und Taxis 169
I am reluctant: 1909 169

When viewed: January 16, 1922, R. R. Junghanns 172
I personally: January 16, 1922, R. R. Junghanns 172
What presumption: May/June 1905 172
I will not conceal: December 2, 1913, Reinhard Sorge 173
Please keep in mind: May 14, 1911, Marlise Gerding 173
Who can be sure: November 8, 1915, Lotte Hepner 174
In purely spiritual matters: June 4, 1914, Reinhard Sorge 174
Never has religion: February 3, 1921, Inga Junghanns 175
Joy is: December 5, 1914, Marianne von Goldschmidt-
  Rothschild 175
Among all: August 30, 1920, Baladine Klossowska 175
The reality: January 31, 1914, Ilse Erdmann 175
There are times: January 19, 1912, Marie von Thurn und Taxis 176

ON GOODNESS AND MORALITY: *Nothing Good, Once It Has
  Come into Existence, May Be Suppressed*

Nothing good: 1907 179
Actually there is: January 17, 1923, August Faust 179
Nothing makes: January 31, 1922, Inga Junghanns 179
To promote: August 28, 1915, Annette de Vries-Hummes 179
When the right help: May 20, 1921, Nanny Wunderly-Volkart 179
Out of all these: February 14, 1904, Ellen Key 180
To preserve tradition: March 30, 1923, Leopold von Schlözer 181
I long for individuals: September 22, 1918, Marie von Bunsen 182
An individual: August 6, 1919, Aline Dietrichstein 182
But there is: December 20, 1922, Mathilde Vollmoeller 182
The kinds of experiences: August 30, 1919, Lisa Heise 183
Violence is: November 15, 1918, Erich Katzenstein 183
Simply having plans: January 28, 1922; Rolf von Ungern-
  Sternberg 183
If human beings: August 6, 1919, Aline Dietrichstein 183
The kind of religiosity: August 20, 1908, Eva Cassirer 184